This book is for you

Charmaine

because I care about your life

Happy
Shopping
Rim asi

Charmane

Maybe
Shopping
We can

# Shopping for...™
# a MAN

The Ultimate Woman's Guide
to Dating a Really Great Guy

# Lumari

BLUE
STAR

For information on licensing or special sales, please contact Lumari at contact@Lumari.com.

Library of Congress Control Number: 2016921126
Trade Paperback ISBN: 978-0-9679553-3-9
E-book ISBN: 978-0-9679553-7-7

Printed in the United States of America
Book Design and Cover Art: Lumari

Published by Blue Star

Contact:
Lumari
BLUE STAR NETWORK
7 Avenida Vista Grande, Suite 113
Santa Fe, New Mexico 87508

 BLUE
STAR

Set the tone and energy for your
shopping and dating success.

Download your FREE
READY TO SHOP visualization

ShoppingForaMan.com

# Acknowledgments

I would like to express my gratitude to the many who provided support, talked things over, read, wrote, offered comments, allowed me to quote their remarks and assisted in the editing and proofreading.

To my beloved husband, Peter Bried, who makes my heart dance, my eyes smile and makes me laugh out loud every day. Thank you for the true love, partnership and fun in every lifetime and I am in honor and gratitude that we continue on this creative journey together. And Peter, thanks for producing my brilliant audio books.

To Lyz Meyer, my dearest friend, appreciation for deep friendship and for your comments and encouragement to bring this book forward. Thank you to Lynn Swanson for friendship and final editing of this book. Your insights and guidance were so valuable. Thank you Donna Kozak for your private coaching and the first edits of this book. Your encouragement and words of wisdom helped get this book out into the world.

I also want to thank the people who inspired me to write this book, to be courageous and to share the best of myself with you.

There are very special people whose work, words and wisdom inspired me. I've included their quotes in this book and want to express my gratitude for their permission and graciousness. Many joyful thanks to Steve Jobs, Oprah, Alan Simpson, Stacy London, Marie Kondo, Danielle LaPorte, Nina Garcia, Heidi Klum, Greg Behrendt, Marie Forleo, Taylor Swift, Lady Gaga, Patti Stanger, Jack Canfield, Deepak Chopra, Michelle Obama, Donna Karan, Sheryl Sandberg, Phil McGraw, Peter F. Drucker, Nora Ephron and Billy Crystal, and Michael Buble.

# CONTENTS

The Power Is in Your Hands

Finding that wonderful man, to have and to hold, is shopping. Dating is shopping. It's just that basic. This is great news. Women are trained shoppers. Discover how shopping for a man can change your dating habits and success.

Dismiss the Myths and Get Real

Break apart the illusions, myths and assumptions you hold about men, dating and life that stand in the way of finding a really great guy, and have fun doing it. Prepare to enter the "Great Galactic Shopping Mall Of Love."

The TOSS, HOLD, KEEP System

Learn the "Toss, Hold, Keep" method that will help you sort, clean and reorganize your dating ideas. Get rid of the old styles, ripped clothes and hand-me-down criteria about men and dating that clutter your closet and begin to make room for your shopping success.

Creating Your Shopping for a Man List

Don't get distracted by the display model. How to make the most powerful shopping list of the attributes, and qualities you need for a really great guy. Learn about The 7 Crucial Items you must have on your Shopping list

# PREFACE

My journey to writing this book seems a surprise and it also seems somehow pre-determined. This is about shopping for a man, and it may seem a departure from my work as an intuitive life and business coach, transformational healer, spiritual teacher and psychic consultant. Surprise, this book is all about the system and methods I used to find and date the most amazing man who is my true beloved. What I discovered is that *Shopping For A Man* is another way I can help women, help you, learn new ways to grow, flourish and be yourself, while dating. In this book, I share fun, fabulous tips, teachings, meditations and more to help you find and date a great guy and be a Shopping Queen. It's about shopping and I love shopping.

Actually, I began my real shopping career when I was four years old. My mother, Esta, took me with her whenever she went shopping and I have to say I learned at the feet of a master.

My mother loved to shop. Almost every Saturday, we would wake up early, get on the subway and go to Filene's basement in Boston. Filene's basement was the original bargain shopping destination. Long before Marshalls, TJ Maxx, Saks Off 5th and any of the other discount and outlet stores, Filene's basement was it. High-end designer fashions and brand name items were seriously discounted. Women would line up hours before a sale and rush the door. The shopping frenzy was astounding. These are sales of legend. This is one of my earliest playgrounds.

I remember sitting under the dress racks holding the clothes that we were going to buy. I remember looking up at my mother, seeing the intensely joyful look on her face as she found the perfect top, the right suit and the most amazing shoes at the best prices. My mother would commandeer a spot by the mirror, grab a whole rack of clothes and organize everything by size and markdown with unsurpassed expertise. Then she would school me. She would tell me why she picked it, what worked and what didn't and then assemble different outfits.

I learned how to recognize and check for top quality, personal preference and how to be quick and decisive. And my mother didn't just shop for herself. She knew every person's size and preference, so if she saw something they might like she got it. Then they would come into our house and our living room became a boutique. All of us girls and our moms would try on the clothes my mother brought home. Imagine trying on clothes in a room of ten girls and our mothers. When everyone shares their opinion and votes on your outfit, you learn what looks good. We'd choose and purchase what we liked. Then next week, mom and I would go to the store and return the rest.

My shopping education wasn't just about clothes. We went to the best galleries on Newbury Street and the gallery owners would tell us about their artists and share about the brilliance of each painting and sculpture. We went to the museums and my mother would ask me questions about the paintings, so I could put that art education to work. We went to design showrooms, home showrooms and anywhere there were really great things to see and purchase.

My mother would never go to someone's house without a gift. We were far from rich, but my mother created her own mini gift shop in the little upstairs bedroom. She had crystal bowls, beautiful candles, serving pieces, special soaps, towels, linen tablecloths and more, plus all the gift-wrap and ribbons to make a gorgeous gift. When you asked Esta (and Eddie my dad) to your home for dinner, she arrived with a set of hostess towels or a serving piece from her mini gift shop. She knew everyone's taste, the colors of their home and even their kids sizes and birthdays. She was always prepared. When I say I learned to be an expert shopper at the feet of a master, I mean it.

I didn't really distinguish this skill or apply my shopping expertise to dating, until I had dated enough guys to know that I was missing something. I mean I certainly was a strong, independent woman. I was a self-supporting artist and sculptor with a fabulous loft space on the wharf. I was selling my work and showing in museums. Did I really need a man in my life? Did I need or even want a husband? Was it worth the trouble and heartache? Finding a guy and dating was painful, discouraging and too much work.

Then, one day, I had an epiphany that changed my life. I realized that dating is shopping. Well, if dating is shopping, I can do that. Shopping for a man? I love shopping! I LOVE SHOPPING! I am a skilled, expert shopper.

So, I put my shopping skills to the test. I developed a whole "shopping for a man" system just for myself. I went over every detail and promised myself I would follow my own shopping rules. I wrote my lists and remembered all the lessons and skills my mother taught me. I just applied them to men and life instead of clothing, housewares and design. I knew if a man had the qualities I needed or if he didn't. And, if he didn't he wasn't the guy for me. I relaxed and had fun.

My "shopping for a man" system worked. Through my own diligence and my own shopping methods, I met an amazing guy who is now my husband. I had a very detailed and exhaustive list of qualities, traits and more that I wanted, needed and appreciated in a man. I wrote them down and didn't censor myself. I stuck to my entire plan and I found the man I truly, enduringly love. And he feels the same about me. We have a relationship that is truly blessed.

Once I successfully shopped for a man and found the man of my dreams, I put away the list. Ah, but the Divine had other things in mind. My clients continued to ask about their dating choices, and I would ask them some of the questions I had asked myself when I was shopping for a man. These special questions and the guidance I shared helped so many clients have epiphanies and insights about themselves, dating and men.

I kept on receiving inner guidance that I had to put this fun wisdom into words. The idea and teachings for this book kept on infiltrating my thoughts. I kept on receiving the guidance to write it down. Finally, I just said "Okay, I'll write the book."

I first wrote *Shopping For A Man* in 1996 to explore and document my own personal process in dating. What did I do? What did I shop for? How did I know what was right for me? My own shopping for a man self-guidance helped me discover more about myself and learn to be the woman I am, so I could find a really great guy who was right for me. I wrote it, copyrighted it and then let it sit. I really didn't know what to do with this book at the time, so I filed it away. I continued my spiritual and intuitive coaching practice and leading workshops, while writing spiritual books.

Then, a short time ago, this book came back to me. My dear mother told me, "It's time to bring this book out into the world." My mother has passed from this world to the great beyond, and still true to her being, told me I had to get this book out. "Women are waiting for this book. Think of how many women you can help. Think about the beautiful women you can help to find love and still be true to themselves. It's time." Well, if my mother is calling from beyond to tell me to expand the book and get it out there, then that's what I have to do.

I was lucky to have strong, honest, loving and courageous women in my family and in my life. It's always about inner-truth and empowerment for me. I delight in empowering women. I help and coach women and men to be true to their gifts, embrace their purpose and then take action in the world from that beautiful, unique, inner space so they can achieve greater success in all areas from the inside out.

So, I listened to my mother. I did what Esta told me to do. I still wasn't sure whether my ideas about shopping and dating would resonate with anyone, but I rediscovered my book, edited it and added lots more fun, meditations and teachings, and stories from some of my clients.

Now, I'm ready to share this with you. I'm ready to teach you and train you, how to shop for a man.

If you want a real relationship, this is a fun and powerful way of learning what works, gaining real skills and then, going shopping!

Oh Ma, what a surprise! I took all the lessons I learned from years of your shopping training to whole other level. I am using my expert skills to teach women how to go shopping for a man. I know you are smiling down from heaven and laughing!

***We're going shopping!***

# INTRODUCTION

Are you ready to find a fabulous guy for a magnificent long-term, monogamous relationship and have fun doing it? It's time to go shopping! As your shopping expert guide and guru, I reveal the new secrets to help you find and date that fabulous guy, the love of your life. You will finally burst the illusions about dating, so you can date an appropriately great guy, find deeper meaning in your life, get ready for true love and have fun doing it.

Everything is Shopping! That's the deep truth, the hidden secret, I'm sharing with you that will help you find the man of your dreams in a joyful, discerning and powerful way. It's fun! Shopping is fun. I'll make dating fun, too. That's why you need this training and expertise. Do you want to find the best guy who is right for you in so many ways?

### *If you love men and you love shopping, this is your book!*

And even if you don't know much about expert shopping, yet, my book will train you how to find and date a great guy, using my special shopping training and methods.

*Shopping For A Man* is a fabulously fun and powerful guide filled with tools, teachings and techniques that will eliminate the unlikely men and lead you to really great guys. They're out there. You simply need to discover the best tools to understand who you are, what you really need and how to stay focused, so you can find that great guy, that amazing man, The One.

You will learn how these fun and powerful methods will
- break apart the illusions you have about yourself and about men that stand in your way to finding a really great guy
- get rid of outmoded ideas and beliefs to make room for your shopping success
- keep your clear focus amidst the bargains and knock-off's
- learn the powerful clues and signs so you know the difference between fabulous and flawed

And then, *Shopping For A Man* gives you even more training, tools and teachings to help you get a closer look at who this guy really is, so you can see what he's made of and whether he is a perfect fit for you in your life.

Read this book from front to back and follow the expert advice, steps and guidance I share with you. *Shopping For A Man* removes the fluff and gives you true expertise so you can find and date really great guys and choose the one who is perfect in your life, and ensure that you are perfect for each other. Each chapter of this book has visualizations and exercises, so you can really have fun uncovering and letting go of your own assumptions. It's time to embrace and honor your own shining qualities. Check out ShoppingForAMan. com for special worksheets, resources, links and downloads..

Wait, there's more. An added benefit of this book, is that you will become an expert shopper. Yes, I know my book is about finding a great guy to love forever. *Shopping For A Man* also gives you powerful tips about shopping for just about anything. Remember everything is shopping! So, you'll also be able to start to apply these teachings and techniques to even more in your life.

**It's time to go Shopping For A Man!**

# DEDICATION

To Esta, my mother, who taught me everything about shopping.

Thank you Ma, for Filene's basement and Newbury Street. Thank you for teaching me how to look at the merchandise and know what was really a deal and what was a waste of time and money. Thank you for schlepping me to every store, for the ice cream sundaes after a long day shopping and wonderful conversations. Whether it was fashion, clothes, art or home design, it was always fun and invigorating. Shopping with you was an art and a sport. And I still use and treasure those skills today.

And thanks Ma, for showing me what a great relationship could be. You and Dad had one and showed me that love is grand. Through good times and hard times, I could always see the love in your eyes and know the love in your hearts. Actions spoke louder than words, but the loving words were always spoken, too.

I dedicate this book to you, Esta, and to everyone who is ready for the love of their life and the relationship to last the tests of time.

P.S. Dad, I'm not forgetting you. I know all about car shopping and negotiating from you! You were a perfect example of a loving husband and a great dad. But, after all, this is about shopping for a man!

P.P.S. Peter, my beloved! You are the best, the light, the love, the man of my dreams and my life. I am blessed by who you are every moment of my life. Thanks for shopping with me!

CHAPTER 1

# DATING IS SHOPPING
## The Power Is in Your Hands

Shopping. Beautiful stores filled with wonderful things, and everything thing there just waits for you to buy it. Yes! All of the dresses hang on the racks, in colors and materials just begging you to touch them. Little cotton tee shirts, piled neatly on the table, conjure summer days in the garden. Shoes! Oh, those strappy, brown leather sandals that will look perfect on your small feet. Over there are those flowing silk dresses in irresistible colors. What about that sexy velvet top, the one that slips just off the shoulder?

No one ever told you that when you are out in the world, looking for the love of your life, you are really shopping. No one mentioned it, did they? Well, you are. You are shopping for a man. Finding that wonderful man, to have and to hold, is shopping. It's just that basic.

This is great news. Women are trained shoppers. We're good at it. Shopping is in our DNA. Actually, we're the experts. We can be highly discerning about the quality, the fit and the longevity of a purchase. Usually we know when we're buying a fad or a classic. We learn how to shop for great food in the supermarket. We discover the best boutiques. We know about the designers and interiors and the food and we shop for them all the time.

### So, now you know the secret.
### "Dating Is Shopping."

Shopping is fun. Dating can be fun, too. Seriously. You can meet some wonderful guys. You can connect with men who are ready and happy to find a fabulous gal like you. And, even if you don't find your soul mate right away, you can still have fun dating. Surprised? Good!

In the old view of dating, you're trying to figure out how to get the guy. Where do you go? How do you connect? Will you ever find the right guy? Do you have to change yourself to attract a boyfriend? This leads to fear, desperation, loneliness and insecurity. Well, that's not fun.

Shopping is fun and I'm going to show you how to find your love and have fun dating. It's all about shopping and I'm going to reveal the secrets, so you can become a shopping expert and date the right guy for you.

Are you trying to find a really great guy, a fabulous match and partner for your life and having no success? Do you wonder where all the good guys are? You're out there looking and nothing is happening. No love. No great guy.

Are you dating, but finding the guys you meet just don't measure up? They don't get you at all. You look around and see you've lowered your standards and still the guys are just not right for you.

Are you wasting months on guys who don't want a committed relationship, who really don't want anything more than a casual relationship? Have you spent years waiting for a man to propose when he was never really going to, he was just leading you on? That can be crushing. No matter what your age, being single, lonely and looking for love is truly painful. Loving and losing can hurt far more than never loving at all.

Actually, most women and girls I know just don't know how to find a great guy. All of these thousands of years of dating on our planet, and there are still millions of women and girls, just like you, who are hurt and suffering from the dating game. They receive advice from all different sources, but it doesn't help. It doesn't help them find someone who will cherish, support, respect and love them and create a real partnership together.

If this isn't bad enough, you have a hidden problem. This problem is pervasive. It definitely annoys me. What is this hidden problem facing you? Many of the dating gurus do not value your unique gifts, individuality and your life. Okay, I know that's a bold, sweeping generality, but a lot of the dating advice today is telling you that you have to change to please a guy. They are telling you that you need to change yourself in order be datable, loveable and marriageable. Some of the gurus advocate that women and girls have to change who they are and what they want in life just to find, appeal to, and then get the guy. So, not only do you have difficulties finding a great guy who is honest, caring, fun, smart and more, but also too many people tell you that you can't be yourself and get a great guy.

Sorry, gals, this is crap. How are you going to find a man who really loves you and is right for you, if you have to play games, change who you are and try to fit in to a guy's idea of what he wants? Dating is shopping. If you wear a size 6 dress, there's no reason and no point in shopping for a size 12. He is not going to be the right guy for you. If you have to be quiet and soften your opinions, try to be alluring, change your interests, do what men want, change how you look, how you dress, how you talk, then you are not being yourself. You won't find, date and have a real, honest, powerful, supportive and loving relationship that lasts, if you're trying to be someone you're not just to get the guy. If you are a big and beautiful woman, there is no benefit to shopping in the petite section. You are not being genuine. That's like being a casual jeans and tee shirt kind of gal, and advisors are trying to put you into a tutu and tiara!

You may not see the devious nature of this advice. Under the message of helping you, they are telling you that you are not good enough to get a guy unless you change yourself into something else, someone else. You're a Keds kind of gal and they are telling you that the only way to get a guy is to wear Jimmy Choo's.

Can you imagine how painful it would be to try to be someone else, and then have to play that game for the rest of your life so you can have love and be loved? The hidden message is that you are not good enough, that you cannot connect with a great guy without changing yourself to be an image of what is desirable. They are saying that you are doomed to be alone and isolated, without a great love in your life, because you are who you are. What kind of 21st Century advice are they giving our fabulous girls and women if they tell them that they are not good enough on their own?

Can you feel the pain of that? Can you feel the pain, sadness, confusion and insecurity that results when people tell you that who you are is not good enough, not worthy of a relationship, because you don't fit into a stereotype that someone made up? When the advice you get, the books you read and the pseudo-wisdom tells you that you can't have love and a great guy because you don't have the beauty, qualities, personality and malleability that men want, they are telling you you're not good enough. This is not a good way to start to find a great guy. Just from this negative advice, you are feeling more insecure and unworthy. They are telling you: You have to change to get the guy. You have to be someone else. You have to fake it to make it. You have to be a cheap stereotype of what men want in a woman, in order to get a guy. That's playing a dating game. Love and life partnership are not a game. Where is your empowerment?

This approach also suggests that what you want in a guy is less important than what the guy wants in a gal. No matter what you have to do or change, it's you who has to change to get a great guy. Remember: If you love the flair, fun and flirty color of Betsey Johnson's fashion, then shopping at the GAP is not going to be fulfilling. If you love the casual, comfy, laid back clothes in the GAP, then Betsey Johnson's fashion will be too much.

### *If you love men and you love shopping, this is your book!*

Dating is shopping for a man. When you go shopping for a man, you will meet a guy who complements your life. If you love high-end fashion and cutting edge design, then Target, as fabulous a store as it is, will not have the styles you want. That's a good thing.

Shopping is all about getting what works for you. When you have shopping expertise, you know your style and what works for you. Shopping for a man means the more in tune you are with yourself, the better you can explore the world of shopping.

*When you think of dating as shopping, it's much more fun!*

## IT'S BEST TO BE THE BEST YOU!

This book is not about changing you, just so you can get a guy. This book is not about playing games. For thousands of years, society has told girls and women that they have less value then men. You have to change to please the guy, but the men can make all the decisions and set the course. You have to follow their lead, because women are less than men.

Really think about this, because it pertains to the advice you get from other people. Society as a whole still thinks women are less valuable than men. Women get paid less then men, while doing the same job as men. On a whole, women make 21 percent less than men doing the same jobs. There is still a glass ceiling preventing women from reaching high-level positions. In some countries, women cannot drive, women cannot vote, they cannot choose their husband, they cannot own property and they cannot get an education.

Okay, I can go on and on from here, but my point is that you are not less than a man. You are great. You are a blessing. You have deep beauty within yourself and a guy is really lucky that you have those qualities and gifts and are willing to share your time, and maybe your life with him.

You are valuable. I value you. I want you to value yourself and discover what you need and want in a guy and a relationship that will bring you love, joy, wisdom, connection, support, freedom, passion and more. That's why I'm sharing my unique and fun guide to dating. When you know dating is shopping and you learn the skills of a Power Shopper, then you know the power is in your hands.

We're going shopping!

*"Your time is limited, so don't waste it living someone else's life. Don't let the noise of others' opinions drown out your own inner voice. And most important, have the courage to follow your heart and intuition. They somehow already know what you truly want to become. Everything else is secondary."*
Steve Jobs

## GROWTH VS. CHANGE

We all have the opportunity to grow. Growth is evolution through awareness and action. Personal growth, development, maturity and openness to being a better you, is a perfect path to tread. When I say, "It's best to be the best you," I mean recognize and appreciate who you are.

Change is to alter or adapt. When you change yourself to adapt to what other people think will help you fit in, it's not growth. It's a sad manipulation of your spirit and self-esteem. Don't change to please someone else, to fit in or to get a guy. Growth is not about changing to become someone else's idea of you. It's a deep inner growth so you can be fulfilled in your life.

What do you do to be the best you? You follow your passion. You follow your heart. If following your passion means that you want to do something unusual, great! If following your heart means that you feel like an artist, or want to volunteer to help others, or you really want to be an engineer and design green materials for the future, that is fabulous.

You evolve when you want to grow and be the best you. You move into a greater part of your own self. Your dreams and ideas become more real. You change within yourself and grow more beautiful. You can read spiritual and empowering books so you can learn from the wisdom of others and see if that fits your dreams and makes your heart happy. You can do meditation, visualizations and have real goals you want to accomplish. You can take extra courses in subjects that interest you. You can find other people, mentors, coaches or friends that have more experience, so you can grow and learn from their wisdom.

Everything you do, to be the best you, will make you shine inside and out. If you want to learn more about the social graces, or learn better ways to communicate, that's being a better you. If you want to update your looks and get a glam makeover, that's perfect. If you recognize that you can look better, that your make-up could use some tweaking and your wardrobe is just not flattering you, then do it! If updating your style, your training and your career will give you joy, confidence and new opportunities, go for it. That's not changing who you are to suit someone else's idea. That's you, ready to take the next steps to improve your life.

In my work as a psychic consultant and life coach, I know that my clients who are striving to be better, to open themselves to more in life are usually happier and more successful. Let your mind and heart expand. Dream your biggest dreams and then follow them. Have the courage to follow your heart, pursue your passion and do what you love.

I'm writing this book to give you the real tools to help you discover ways to date and choose guys in a whole new way. I want you to have the power, the skill and the wisdom to know who you are and find a partner who will love and appreciate you and fit into your life. Each chapter is filled with guidance, tips and visualizations to help you be a Shopping Queen.

## Everything Is Shopping!

The heart and soul of this book is, Dating Is Shopping. The fun part of dating is actually shopping, but it's all shrouded in mystery that does not give you power.

It's time to gain real expertise that will give you the power, skill and readiness to go shopping for a man. Let's start right now.

### Let's go shopping!

# Visualization and Affirmation
# READY TO SHOP

The Ready To Shop Visualization and Affirmation sets the tone and energy for your shopping and dating success. It will help you be open to new possibilities and sharpen your shopping skills, so you can be a savvy shopper.

To be most effective with the visualizations in my book, there's a little set up to help you be more clear and open. I call the process of getting into a clear space in your mind, energy and heart, 'centering.' Centering helps you be more clear, put aside distractions and get in touch with a deeper part of yourself. The more you practice centering the better you'll get. You can use centering for everything from taking tests, to performing, to just listening and learning. Plus this centering exercise is perfect to use to start your day, change activities and be really clear and present in your life.

Here is the "3 Steps To Centering" exercise to quickly prepare yourself to get ready and be successful in shopping for a man. Use this centering exercise before each of the visualizations and affirmations and you'll be more focused and clear to create greater success and harmony.

# 3 Steps To Centering

Here are the 3 Steps To Centering exercise.
Do the 3 Steps To Centering exercise at any time to clear your mind,
relax your body and eliminate distractions and stress.

### *1. BE IN THE QUIET.*

Please, just for a few moments, shut off your phone, computer etc.
and give yourself some quiet space. Claim some space  and time to
be calm and at ease.

### *2. SIT COMFORTABLY.*

Sit on the sofa, a cushy chair, maybe even pillows on the floor. You
want to be relaxed, but not in position where you'll fall asleep.

### *3. BREATHE DEEPLY.*

Take several deep breaths. Let your shoulders and body relax.
You are here, now, breathing, calm, at ease and being you.

Continue to breathe slowly and deeply.
Inhale to the count of four. Exhale to the count of four.
Inhale to the count of four. Exhale to the count of four.

Let your thoughts drift. Keep your mind clear and unfocused. That
means don't think about anything specific, just let yourself space out.
Do this for 2 - 5 minutes until you feel calmer and more focused.
Then begin the visualization. You can do this meditation at any time
to regroup and feel centered and calm. You can also do this meditation in the mornings before your day, at breaks during work, when
you're stressed and need to collect yourself, and at any time day or
night, just because it feels really good.

# Visualization: Ready To Shop

Take a deep breath.
Imagine an amazing shopping mall. Everything is shining and new and fresh. The lights really complement the different stores and styles. The music is fun and you almost feel like dancing.

You have your great shopping bag. You are wearing the shoes to cruise. You're in a great mood, feeling optimistic and happy and ready. You are ready to shop.

Now, you look toward the sign above you. It says, "The Great Galactic Mall Of Love."

You're in the right place. You're here at the perfect time. There are fabulous men everywhere. There are so many of them and they are all looking to fall in love with a great gal like you.
You're not going to pick a guy today. You're going to delight in the possibility that there are great guys out there and you are ready to meet a wonderful man.

Take a slow deep breath and then say these affirmations. You can say them out loud or silently.

> I am ready to go shopping for a man.
> I am ready to put aside my fears, insecurities and concerns about dating and men.
> I am open to finding a great guy who will love me, appreciate me and celebrate me for who I am.
> I am ready to learn what I need, what I want, and what will complement my life.
> I am ready to learn all of the shopping skills.
> I am ready to go shopping for a man.

Now, smile.
Take an imaginary selfie of you in a happy pose under the sign, "The Great Galactic Mall Of Love."

Feel the new you. You are positive, strong and ready to see yourself and dating in a new way.

# Affirmation and Intention:
# READY TO SHOP

Use this affirmation whenever you like to support your new under-standing and positive energy and outlook. Try it right now and feel your new energy. You can have more fun, freedom and a real posi-tive mind-set.

Take a slow deep breath.
Smile and say,

**_"I am ready to go shopping for a man."_**

Perfect. Just relax and when you are ready, open your eyes.

Congratulations. "The Great Galactic Mall Of Love" is now open and your shopping training will begin.

CHAPTER

2

# BUSTING YOUR ILLUSIONS
## Dismiss the Myths and Get Real

Once you know that dating is shopping, the rest is easy. After all, you've been shopping all of your life. You have all of the skills you need to find the perfect partner. The trick to this is that you haven't applied any of the major shopping rules to dating. Actually, you may not even know there are shopping rules. It's time to get real. In the "Great Galactic Shopping Mall Of Love," everything is there and you can have what you want. All you have to do is make a selection.

Tricky? Of course. "The Great Galactic Mall Of Love" is filled with wonderful things. Every style, every color, every shape and every size you can imagine are all lined up in their pretty displays, just waiting to be wrapped up and go to a nice home. Where do you start? Do you know what you want? What department are you heading to? Are you prepared for a day of shopping? When you shop for a major purchase, you do some research. You examine your needs and wants. You check your budget. You decide what to buy. Then you check the stores for good quality, well-made merchandise. Finally, you bring that fabulous item home. These same skills will help you find the man that you want, the perfect fit!

You need some basic ideas of what you want to shop for and whether it pays to buy it. Don't worry. Most women are fantastic shoppers. After you cruise for a while, you know if the vegetables are fresh or not. You can tell stale bread. You know the smell of a fish that stayed too long in the market. Well, shopping for a man is the same thing. Some of them are stale. Some of them have been in the case a little too long and they have that fishy smell. All you have to do is recognize that odd smell and you'll never buy that fish!

Do you know why no one ever told you to shop for a man? Do you know why you didn't think of this yourself? It's because everyone has illusions about the perfect man and the perfect love. Illusions are the stories you think are true, but they are not. These stories are woven into every aspect of life. Everyone agrees that they are facts of life. Wake up! Romance, love and relationships are wrapped in mythologies. The social conditioning of your past taught you to think in certain ways. The ideas from the media, your friends and family, and the dating scene are mostly based on romantic illusions. You are conditioned to think and respond in a certain way. It's not real. The myths of romance, of falling in love, are just nice stories.

Collectively, we create the script. We choose from among all of the stories and decide which suit our time and culture. Then everyone buys it. The narratives are wonderful. You can sink into a comfortable chair and relax in the fantasy, but these stories don't give you any skills to strengthen your life and make powerful choices. The legend about the tall, handsome man who whisks you away into a life of love and luxury is a very creative tale. It may have happened once or twice, but it isn't anything you can bank on or wait for.

Books may fill their pages with dashing men who rescue frail women, but how many times have you seen this in your neighborhood? Did you ever meet them? Your family showed you how they feel about men. Your older sisters told you what men are like. If you believe the myths and illusions, you live your life inside them.

*There are a lot of myths about dating.*
*Fortunately, you're not looking for a mythical creature.*
*You're looking for a real man.*
*Drop the myths and go shopping.*

There are myths about each racial group. There are myths about all the different cultures. There are myths about the sexes. There are fully constructed ideas about how people in each social group act. They aren't true. This same social conditioning tells you what women are like. In the movies, women are often helpless victims of the world. They don't have choices. They can only react to situations. They are victims of society, men, family and of themselves. They can be strong, but only with anger, to avenge the villain and protect themselves or their children. This makes a great drama. You can sit on the edge of your seat in a movie theatre and be fully captivated, but do you want to live this one out? Do you think this is really true? Do you think that all women are like that? Are you? Isn't there so much more to women than this quick glance into a make believe world? You bet there is!

Well, the media, your family, friends and community hold these images as real. They present them as absolute facts. Then everyone buys these stories, thinking they are real. They aren't. If you think that they are, then you have no choice but to act them out. There is no truth about how women are. There is no truth about how men are. It's all a conditioned response. Some men nurture. Some don't. Some women are bold. Others are not. Each person has hundreds of unique qualities. Break up the myths and you can see the truth. Break up the illusions and you have freedom and choice. You bought the illusions. It's time to bust them! Now I'm sharing my secret with you. Dating is Shopping.

As an intuitive coach and spiritual teacher, I always receive Divine guidance and I pay attention to it. One day, during a very powerful, hours-long meditation about life, spirit and love, I received the message, "EVERYTHING IS SHOPPING." I love this message and applied it to my life. It still makes me smile. I saw that many of my women clients were struggling with finding a great guy. They were lost in the fantasies, but they didn't have a resource, a clear path to put it all in perspective. My main focus is full personal development. That means total guidance and healing so you can live your soul purpose, follow your destiny and create a rich fulfilling life. My focus and gift is helping clients live inspired in their personal growth, business and spiritual life. Since many of my women clients were struggling in the dating world, I shared my ideas and system of shopping for a man with them. I shared titbits of wisdom and it made a huge shift for them. I still have clients calling me, reminding me of what I said to them about their relationship and how much it helped.

Rachel has been my client for many years. I've seen her success grow beyond her dreams. She is an exciting entrepreneur working in green, eco-friendly products. Most of our intuitive coaching sessions focus on her personal growth and business success. She wasn't really interested in dating or marriage. She was happy and fulfilled.

Then one day she told me she was ready to find a guy. She was ready to start dating again, but … she wasn't excited, she was nervous. All the bad dates and relationships were swimming in her thoughts. Initially our conversation was more about the failures, the breakups and the pain.

After she shared her fears, I asked her, "Do you like to go shopping?"

Without hesitation she said. "Yes. I love shopping."

So, I shared my ideas about dating and shopping. She was the first gal I told.

She got so excited. "Tell me more. Tell me everything."

This is what I said:

*Dating is shopping. When you are looking for the love of your life, you're really shopping for a man.*

I was glad to share my insights, the process and everything I knew about shopping for a man. She was thrilled. Her whole attitude changed about dating, and finding a great guy. It wasn't an impossible feat. It was a shopping trip! She's a fabulous shopper, and now, she's married to the love of her life.

So, here I am, years later realizing that it's time to share this with you. It's time to show you how shopping for a man is the key to finding, dating and recognizing a great guy. This book is filled with fun and practical training to help you understand what you really need, how to shop for a man. I'm listing lots of buyer beware tips so you know what to avoid and how not to fool yourself. You'll discover and even heal some of the illusions so you can find a great guy and create a wonderful life together.

To be an effective, powerful shopper, you have to prepare. In order to find, examine and buy the perfect item, you have to be clear and calm. This attitude is important. You need to know what you want and how to go about finding it. Shopping for a man is not like picking up a few things at the supermarket. You can't just pop in, grab some milk and bread, and leave. Choosing a man is a major purchase. There's prep work. Do your preparations and shopping is easy.

The first step in preparation is to re-examine the truths you hold. Clean up the illusions and myths and you can do it. No one really believes that if they use the right deodorant, men will fall at their feet professing undying love and devotion. No one expects those designer labels will get him or her the job. Those little breath mints can help your mouth taste fresher, but if you haven't brushed your teeth in four weeks, it won't matter. It sounds great in advertising, but you know it isn't true. You have the same kind of illusions about men and relationships. You know the truth, but you believe the fantasy. The hype is everywhere. Break up the hype and you can be a clear, efficient, happy shopper.

You feel ready to get a great man. The time is ripe. Your engines are in gear. To get to the mall and get the exact purchase you seek, you have to shake up the illusions and GET REAL. You need to clear out the assumptions you have that don't work for you. You have to be ready to look at those ideas you have and bust them to pieces. Do this and the rest of the prep work, and you will find that great man and have a meaningful relationship. You will know what you want and need. If you don't recognize some of the myths and get clear on what you want, how will you find him? How will you know what you are looking for and whether you actually got it? You want to come home with a man, but so far you're looking for a ghost, an image. Your imagination will not buy you dinner at a lovely restaurant.

*If you shop for a phantom, you come home with empty bags.*

You didn't know that you were shopping for a man, did you? You were out in that amazing mall of life and you didn't see the vast selection. Why? Illusions can block your choices. The only reason you didn't shop for a man before is because you didn't know that you could. You didn't know that dating is shopping. There you were, in a world churning with men and you bought all of the stories instead. You didn't come home with a good man. Why? You've been conditioned to shop by the illusions. If you didn't have those illusions, shopping would be much easier and much more fun.

*"Follow your instincts.*
*That's where true wisdom manifests itself."*
*Oprah*

# THE SIX ILLUSIONS OF COMMERCE

First you need to know what some of the illusions are, so you can toss them out like ripped pantyhose. You know, the ones that have holes in the toes so that every time you put them on you can feel the tip of the shoe. The ones with runs all the way up to Canada and if you ever had to take them off in public you'd be redder than Chanel lipstick? It's time to dig through that lingerie drawer and pull out those ripped pantyhose, those old illusions. Look at them, and toss them into the trash.

You may want to examine some ideas that should go into the trash. Any story that blocks your joy goes into the rubbish. As you read these illusions, ask yourself some questions. Does this sound familiar? Do you hear this phrase or one like it rattling around in your head? Do your friends say it? Do you believe it? Do you assume that it's true? Do you think that any one of these illusions is real? Do they describe what life and men are like? If you believe any one of these illusions, is it helping your life? If you believe it, does it give you joy and power? Do you feel confident and alive from it?

The illusions I'm including here are the most common. They all appear to be true. You've heard them. When you read them, does it make you want to get right out into the world and rejoice? No. These illusions and so many others block your choices and your freedom. You may believe several or all of them. Don't worry. If you see that something is garbage, you know exactly where to put it. That's why you are going to bust them up.

## ILLUSION 1:
## There aren't enough men to go around.

Not true. Total fiction. If you believe this illusion you are a doomed shopper. You have no possibility to find a great man, because there aren't enough for everyone. It's time to forget the media figures of how many men are single and straight and waiting for you. It's hype. Who says that all the good ones are taken? How can that possibly be true? It's not. It's a story.

What about the myth that men don't want committed relationships or that they don't appreciate strong, creative women? Lies. There are plenty of smart men who know a great woman when they see her. Forget about competition. Just drop that conversation. It makes you think that all the women are out there are vying for the attention of that one single man. It's a set up. You end up competing against each other without looking at the man at all. There is no scarcity. You can have what you want. Any belief or idea that says that there is a limit on your love and your choices is a lie.

This belief, that there aren't enough to go around, isn't true. It's a myth and you bought the story. It doesn't give you any power. It makes you feel frantic or hopeless. This is the One-Size-Fits-All dress that you brought home and then looked like a refugee in it. All of that is illusion. That's why there's diversity.

Men are everywhere. The selection is absolutely fabulous! You could never get this selection in Bloomingdales, Neiman's, the Gap or wherever else you shop. Just look around! It's delicious. There are some with suits and brief cases. There are some with cowboy hats and jeans. They are tall or short, dark or light and every possible flavor you can imagine. There is no scarcity. Men are everywhere.

If you go out with the thoughts and beliefs that the store just doesn't carry what you're looking for, you won't find it. It's that simple. You will prove yourself right. If you think that there aren't enough men out there, then you sentenced yourself to be without one. You make this illusion real when you believe it. You live under its shadow. No matter how many men you meet, you won't see them. You just scan the shelves, racks and bins, and know all along that they won't have what you want. Well, with this attitude, you wouldn't see it if it were all lit up and on display in the middle of the store. This is an attitude and belief misnomer.

"The Great Galactic Shopping Mall Of Love" has everything. That's right. It has whatever you want. You're shopping for a man. There are billions of men on this planet and all you want is one. This means that you have an excellent selection of goods to choose from. Anywhere you look there are men just hanging around. They are on display wherever you look. Think of it. Everywhere you look there are fabulous men.

*This is a shoppers dream!*
*The planet is filled with men, and all you need is one!*

## ILLUSION 2:
## There are no good men left.

This is boring and you are whining. This links with the first illusion, but it's more insidious. Illusion One tells you there aren't any, so you don't bother to look. This one, Illusion Two, accepts the fact that there are plenty of men to choose from, but they all come with flaws so large that you can't have one anyway. There is a major flaw and something very wrong with every single one.

Sour grapes. It's a lie.

If you consider that this isn't true, you will notice a bounty of terrific men. There are caring, loving men in every corner. They are sitting in restaurants, bars and out in nature. They are in boardrooms and on farms. They are in factories and stores. They are all over. They want a committed relationship. They want a wonderful woman to share life with them.

*If you think there aren't any good, single men to go around,*
*that's okay. You don't want men that go around!*
*You want a man that sticks around.*

So, if you bought the story that they aren't out there, you've become a very haphazard shopper. You scan the shelves and sigh to yourself that they never have anything good here. You pick up a scarf, maybe a wallet, and even if it looks promising, you forget it and drive home empty handed. If you're under this illusion, that's one way you shop for a man. You don't even consider anyone you meet because you know he won't be good.

This can be even worse: At the store, you pick up something you know isn't you, and buy it anyway. It won't work, it isn't what you want, but at least you have something. It's a waste of money. In this example, you take home a man because he is there. He is breathing. You know there are no good ones. You take what you can get. At least you have one, no matter how bad.

Since you don't think there is anyone out there, you stopped looking for a good man. Now, everywhere you look, all you see is what you can't have. This is not the truth. This illusion will not give you any freedom to choose what you want. You already decided that all the merchandise is horrible, so you're stuck with the dregs. You may not have found the one you want yet, but good men are out there, if you know how to shop. Stop complaining to yourself or anyone else. Get a grip. Get your bag and check book. You bought the wrong idea. Consider it false advertising. Get ready to go to the mall and find someone great.

## ILLUSION 3:
## You have to lower your standards to have a relationship.

Wrong. Lowering your standards means that you have to give up who you are to have a relationship. You deny your feelings and your inner truth, just to be with a man. You disregard yourself, what you hold dear, to have a man who doesn't appreciate the same things you do. What's even worse is that with this illusion, you still think that this relationship will work. You think if you give up what you hold dear, then you can have a relationship. Surprise. How can it work? You didn't honor yourself and what you know to be true. You tossed it all away, just for a man. No chance in the underworld that this will be a match.

Standards are the qualities you live your life by. They are a measure of quality, integrity and value. Your personal standards are your model for comparison. You have qualities that are important to you. You have values that you hold dear. They may come from your personal experience, religious upbringing or your family. These ar your standards.

---

### *Don't lower your standards.*
### *Raise your awareness.*

Do you know what your standards are? You may feel that honesty and responsibility are very important. It's how you live your life. These qualities are important to you. You value them in yourself and in others. You don't lie to or cheat your friends. You won't steal money from the cash register at work. You are an honest person and people can trust you. You take care of your responsibilities, whether they are bills, children or maintaining your home.

If honesty and responsibility are your standards, why would you take home a man who is a liar, just to have a warm body in your bed? This is lowering your standards. You are honest. He is not. You disregarded your values in order to have a man. Bad move.

It's very simple to discover your own values. They are the qualities you hold dear and important. What are your standards? What are the simple guidelines of life that you value? What traits do you appreciate in people? What are your meaningful qualities? What characteristics do you admire in others? When you know your own standards, then you can see them in others.

If you don't find those standards in the man you choose, you have to shop somewhere else. This is your first clue. So, what are you really looking for? If you are looking for an honest, caring man, who will respect and support you, love and honor you, and share your life fully, keep shopping for what you want. You don't have to give up any of your integrity to get a man. It's a broken crock. Don't buy the bowl!

---

*Before you lower your standards, make sure you have them.*

You know what qualities are important. You have values and guidelines for your life. Then you find a virile man who charms your mind and tantalizes your libido. After talking, you know that this man does not appreciate the values that you live by. He boasts about the women in his life. He tells you about the people he ripped off with his clever schemes. He has certain ideas about life that go against your own truth and honesty. Since you think that you have to lower your standards to have a man, you invite him into your life. You just invited disaster into your bedroom.

Sometimes these clues are more evident in the department store. There is a special purse that you want. It's black leather with two small, gold buckles on the front and a short strap. You want it to complement a business suit. It has to be quality material, because you are going to wear it to a very important meeting. Now, when you went to the store you didn't find what you wanted. You looked at everything. Nothing was right. There was a sale in that same department and you brought home a new bag.

What did you buy? You got a large brown, cheap, vinyl beach bag. You figure in your delusion that at least everything will fit inside it and of course it was on sale. Face it. You lowered your standards. You know what you need and what is appropriate for you. You know your size. You know what looks good on you, so why take something that will never work? Because you think that you can't have what you want. Someone said that your standards are too high. You come home with a useless purchase that will annoy you, until you throw it out. Now think: Instead of a vinyl bag, you brought home a vinyl man.

Compromise? Compromise is different. For example, you're shopping for a dress to wear out to dinner. You try on a dress that looks great and fits well. You have shoes to go with it, but the color isn't one you normally wear. You were thinking of something more tailored, but this would definitely work. It still has the classic lines you look for, but it's a little flashier. You know, more style, more pizzazz. It's not what you had in mind, but you are interested. You don't want to attract too much attention to yourself, even though you know you look classy and hot in it. You even have accessories at home to complement the outfit. The other thing uncertain about this dress is that you were looking for deep red and this is purple.

Surprise. This is a keeper. Buy it. That's compromise. You may even find that this changes your appearance for the better. It lifts your spirits. People notice the change. When you lower your standards, you bring home something that you know you don't want. You get a brown vinyl beach bag, instead of a fine leather purse. In a compromise, you get a stylish, well-made dress. The color and design may be different, but you have the quality and fit that you need. You don't give up anything and you may get even more than you dream.

*"If you have integrity, nothing else matters.*
*If you don't have integrity, nothing else matters."*
*Alan Simpson*

Lowering your standards just to have a man at home is going to give you trouble. He will not honor and appreciate you because he doesn't live by the same values. Don't fool yourself. Bring home a man that cheats on his wife with you, and you will have a man that cheats on you. He is a cheater. He doesn't live by a higher standard. Bring home a man who doesn't respect people and he will not respect you.

Compromise gives you greater options in your choices. You decide you want a man with a strong financial income. You compromise when you choose to date a man who doesn't have the financial status you wanted. He is putting himself through college and he works a full time job. He wants to start a new company. He doesn't have much money yet, but he still takes you to dinner.

This man works for his dream. He puts a lot of energy into what he wants and he goes after it. You made a compromise to choose a man who has less money than you wanted, but he puts effort into his life. This is a good compromise. He has the same values as you do; it's just that the money is not in place, yet. He has integrity. He is hard working, but still finds time for you. You didn't lower your standards; you compromised on a minor point.

*If you don't find true standards in the man you choose, you have to shop somewhere else.*

You have to know reality from fantasy when you look at your standards. Look at yourself. Examine your values and needs. You require a real man to help complement your life. He has his strengths and weaknesses. He is out in the world and you can meet him. This is pragmatic shopping. There's no sense in dreaming about some fantasy man you saw on a billboard ad. You want a real man, not some photoshopped picture of magazine imagination. It's delusional. Disneyland is a great place to visit, but you can't really live there.

You have to be open to see who carries the merchandise. Don't bother looking for an honest, high-principled man in a prison cell. He won't be there. You are looking for a Valentino label in K-Mart. Wake up. They don't carry it. You have to be very clear. Is that what you're shopping for? Do you know what you need? Remember those standards that you live by? Keep them. Look for the store that carries what you want. You want a loving man with integrity to share your life. Go to the places that attract those men. Where would a man like this be? What kind of friends would he have? What situations will attract him?

Take a good look at your own standards. Looks change. Styles change. A tall, thin man could gain fifty pounds over the years. Make your selection by values and qualities. Appearances are not inner traits. What kind of treatment, love and support will bring joy and more balance in your life? Is this man honest and responsible? Life goes up and down. Sometimes life packs in a few obstacles. You want a partner to be there with you. You are not looking for some poster boy on the wall to fill your fantasies. Right?

# ILLUSION 4:
## They look good at first. Then they change.

Not true. You have to pay attention. You must want to see the merchandise. When you met him, he was loving and caring. He called you sweet names. He took you to nice places. Then you brought him into your life and he was rude and cold. He changed. He used to be wonderful and now he's horrible.

Does this sound familiar? Sorry. You didn't really look at the outfit before you bought it. You got so excited about the sale. Shopping frenzy. The glitz, the glamour is too much to resist. Each person circling for the right item like buzzards in a desert, made you crazy and impulsive. You fooled yourself. The excitement dazzled and confused you. It looked so good. Of course, it was a superficial look. You didn't really want to see what you were buying.

*The item doesn't change from the store, to the bag,*
*to your home. Neither does a man.*

Here is a good example of shopping frenzy. There's a huge display of chocolates wrapped in gold foil in the center aisle. Oh, they look so delightful and that aroma just fills the air. Every little one is a golden, chocolate jewel, shining in individually wrapped presents. The boxes look like treasure chests of luxury. You picture yourself lounging on the sofa, sipping champagne and eating these delicate morsels of rich delight. Maybe each one has this incredible filling. There is a sign above them, telling you exactly what's inside. You don't look at it. You know you want them. You don't pay attention. You don't care. The glittering paper, the bright light is irresistible. You just have to buy them. So, you do.

All day you think about those chocolates. You can taste that rich chocolate melting in your mouth. You picture yourself lying on the sofa, nibbling these delicate treats in the company of champagne and a very tender video. It is heaven. This will be the most sensual, romantic night of relaxation. You will slip into that satin robe, pull out the crystal glasses and bask in the pure decadence of the night.

You rush home and put the chocolates on the coffee table. After your shower, you wrap yourself in satin. The crystal glass is in your hand and you pour yourself the champagne that you picked up on the way home. Who needs dinner when you have chocolate? You play a movie. The treasure box waits for you on the coffee table, gleaming its soft gold magic.

Finally. You carefully unwrap the individual foil papers and pop one into your mouth. You are in for the shock of your life. Awful. Your face scrunches up in horror and you spit that candy into a napkin. What is that filling? What is in those heavenly little chocolates from that beautiful box? Liver!

### The sign said, "Chocolate-Covered Liver Balls!"

You didn't read the sign. It was big and bold and legible. You got caught up in the joy and romance of it all. You didn't want to know. Now, all you have in that glorious package is chocolate-covered liver balls. Not only does this leave a bad taste in your mouth, it leaves you angry. The sign was right there. Big as life.

The men you date have just as big a sign. They don't change when you take them home. They are that way from the beginning. You don't want to see the truth. You want the romance, the magic. A true magician is very observant and skilled. If you don't look closely, you will not see the illusion.

Say you meet a gorgeous man. He scans the whole room for women, but he sits next to you. He charms you. You do catch him looking around at all the other women in the room, but he chose you, right? When you return from the ladies room, you notice he has several women hanging on him. He dismisses them quickly and returns his attention to you. He is handsome. You are flattered. He could have anyone here. You take him home.

Chocolate Covered Liver Balls. He is vain. He chose you because he knew you would feel flattered. He knew he could charm you. As soon as you left, there were women all over him. He purposely attracted them. He has to have women all the time, and you are one of the many he will have. When you thought he could have any woman in the place, rest assured that he has probably had most of them, already. All of the signs were right there. You didn't want to see them.

When you shop for a man, look closely. Be observant. A man will not change before your eyes. All of the signs are there. You didn't want to see them. You actually avoided looking. Guess what. A man will tell you everything about himself, if you just listen. The key is to listen.

If he tells you that he just couldn't commit to his last eight lovers, he told you he doesn't make commitments. It's a sign. If he speaks about lying, cheating, stealing or fooling someone else, that's who he is. He is a liar and a cheat. If he ignores you and talks to other women instead of you, he just said he doesn't think you're very important. It's obvious. He continually badmouths women and you try to convince yourself that he means them, not you. Wake up. He's telling you everything you need to know. It's right there on the sign next to the chocolate covered liver balls.

## ILLUSION 5:
## I can change him and make it work.

Attention shoppers! This is a mega-illusion. Forget it. Drop it. Don't even put it in your basket! The only thing you can change about a man is his wardrobe. You can help him choose better clothes, but you can't change the man. If you think you can change him, you already see the trouble ahead. It's perfectly clear. You know the signs, and you go after this man anyway. You intentionally ignore every warning. Why? If you wear size seven shoes, how can you possibly think you can buy a size ten and make it work? Sure, you're going to try to be as creative as possible and make it work. You'll stuff the toe. You'll wear big socks. You'll wear a long dress to cover them up. You'll practice walking in these shoes that are so big that you keep on tripping on your own feet. Guess what? They don't fit and never will. So you spent good money for these great looking shoes, thinking you could change them into the right size. No way. What you see is what you get.

Picking a man to change him is buying faulty goods. Men are not fixer-uppers. Here's a good example of this type of thinking. Way across the store is this gorgeous looking sweater. It's exactly the color that you want to go with that darling little skirt you picked up last month. You run for it. Looks fabulous. Then you pick it up. It has a snag on the sleeve. Okay, you'll just pull the thread through, and roll up the sleeves. After all, it's a minor flaw and it is the right color.

Now you look inside. Oh darn. It's a medium and you take a small. That's okay, the baggy look is still in, isn't it? Maybe if you belt it, it will work. You could always buy a new belt, and you just know that if you roll up the sleeves and belt it at the waist, it will still go with that skirt. Won't it?

Time to check the price. Mmmm. It's much more money than you thought. In fact, it's really too expensive. The sweater isn't worth the price they're asking. It's not even a well-known label. You just know it will go perfectly with that skirt, as long as you fix the snag, roll up the sleeves, and buy a new belt. You go to the counter, sweater in hand. The sales person agrees to give you a discount on it because of the snag. Oh, the rapture of the moment. So, you buy it.

What were you thinking? As soon as you saw the snag in the sleeve you should have put it back. It's flawed. Okay, no one is willing to give up that easily, but you know better. You've been shopping before. That snag was your first clue. When you saw that the size was wrong, you should have smiled and walked away. This is a major clue. It's damaged and it doesn't fit. Still, tenacious as you are, you look at the price. Well, girlfriend, this is not a bargain. This is going to cost you dearly.

You already know that these are damaged goods. You know it doesn't fit. Now you know the price is not even worth the merchandise. You have every clue you need to make a smart decision. You buy it anyway. This sweater is not going to change when you bring it home. No amount of love and attention is going to make it fit. Don't buy it. If you absolutely have to go home with something, be very clear that you will return it the next day! Don't get hooked. Who wants to spend good money for a sweater that sits in the closet, looking bad, reminding you that you don't have what you want, and that you paid too much for it?

So, men are the same. You meet an interesting man. In conversation he mentions that he's had a series of twenty jobs in the past four years. He tells you he just hasn't found his calling in life. He asks you to pay for dinner. He keeps on coming over to your house for intimate dinners. You pay for the food, cook the dinner and clean up after him. He continually complains that his life is just not working. Everyone misunderstands him. Still, he just can't make a commitment to a full relationship. After all, he doesn't really know what he should do in life.

Get out! You are not going to help him find himself. He isn't going to find himself because he doesn't want to. He will not change. This is what you brought home. It's not the issue of his jobs. This man is cheap. He told you he doesn't make commitments. It's the truth. He will never make a commitment. He doesn't want to know who he is. Do you think you can change him? No. Don't even take this one home. Leave him in the store.

There are countless stories and endless variations, but if you listen you will hear the truth about him. In this illusion, you know what the flaws are and you think you can change them. Really? Why choose a man who has major problems that he can't work out for himself? You are not going to heal him. Forget about the Clara Barton syndrome. Clara Burton is the nurse who founded the American Red Cross, during the Civil War. So, forget about the Clara Barton syndrome, because you are not out there to heal him and nurse him into a relationship. What are you thinking? Are you looking for a project? If you are, take up sewing!

What if he tells you he used to have a problem making a commitment, or settling down? Now he's seen the light. He used to have difficulty being faithful and his last marriage broke up when he cheated on her. He worked long hours and she said he didn't consider her feelings. It devastated him. This hurt him so much. He realizes he was a jerk. Now he's changed.

Ding, ding, ding, ding. There is a bell going off in your head but you are not listening. He is telling you everything you need to know. This is an alarm clock! Oh, it may sound as if he is confiding in you. He appears so sensitive. You just know that he is ready to change his life after realizing the mistakes that he made. Wake up. It's morning! He just told you enough flaws to set your running shoes in motion.

He is unfaithful. He can't make a commitment. He's whining about it to manipulate you. You can't fill him with enough love that his insecurities and wandering hands will miraculously heal with your devotion. Read the sign. It says, "Fatally flawed goods. Will disintegrate with any criticism, conflict, upset, responsibility, or at the mention of a committed relationship." Finish your drink, get those track shoes on, and run for your life!

## ILLUSION 6:
## If he loves me enough, it will all be okay.

This is a trick. What is "enough"? You don't have enough now, but you will one day, and then everything will work out? How much enough, is enough?

This "enough" word is confusing, because it reveals that you don't, or he doesn't, have what you want. You have an idea, but this isn't it. Enough suggests that if you had more, then it would be fine. Is that really true? Maybe it just isn't there. Maybe it never will be there.

Here's an example of the deceptions of "enough". "I love you, but not enough to make a commitment."

How much love does it take to make a commitment? Is the issue love or commitment? Where can you buy a scale to measure love? When is there enough love to stop evading the question? If it isn't enough, is it really love at all? Maybe he means he'll love you, but only if you don't ask for anything. Does this mean that he loves you when it's convenient? He loves you when it's on his way to the restaurant, but not if he has to drive across town? That's not love. That's location.

Don't bother with this conversation. It is a metaphysical, existential, philosophical approach. Someone is trying to figure out when there is enough love, enough time, and enough bonding. Then, when he figures this out, everything will come together. For this person, there is never enough, because enough suggests that there is a limit. That limit is within him. There has to be more, and he doesn't have it. But the truth is there is no limit to love. Every day love grows, changes, develops and strengthens in ways that are powerful and elusive.

*Enough means that you don't really have what you want.*

Obliterate the word "enough". This word is like looking into an empty abyss. It may be deep but it has no substance. What you want is one high quality purchase. Find a good quality, complementary accessory, and it will last for years. If you have your heart set on a fabulous leather belt, you can have it. If you picked up some vinyl, you better go shopping again. You are looking for a committed relationship. Shop for someone who is looking for the same thing. This man will not worry about how much he needs. He knows that he wants a commitment and that's what he will get.

There are more shopping illusions, but these are a few of the basics to recognize before you get into action. Look inside yourself. Discover what myths you bought as truths. You may be holding several very limiting assumptions about men and relationships that you think are the truth.

Are you in a relationship right now? Check to see if you brought one of these purchases home. Is there a dress in your closet that never fit, is out of style and aggravates you because you didn't get it right? Did you come home with chocolate covered liver balls?

If you still have your receipt, go back to the store and return it. If it's been too long, or you can't even remember why or where you bought it, then give it to the thrift store. If it was good quality material and has just outlived its usefulness, then take it to a women's shelter. After all, what one woman needs another does not. If it was shoddy to begin with, if it is really flawed or damaged, then toss it. Eventually it will become good compost.

*No more chocolate covered liver balls!*

## Visualization and Affirmation

# DITCH THE ILLUSIONS OF COMMERCE

Now that you have a greater understanding of the Six Illusions Of Commerce that interfere with finding a great guy, let's jump right in and bust the illusions so you can have real freedom to go shopping for a man.

Start with the "3 Steps To Centering" exercise.
Every time you do a visualization and an affirmation, use this exercise to get better, more powerful and quicker results.

## Visualization:
## Ditch the Illusions Of Commerce

Take a deep breath.

Picture yourself on the beach by the ocean. It's a beautiful day. The sun is shining. The waves are crashing to the shore. You're barefoot and wiggling your toes in the water as the waves gently ebb and flow. You're in a great mood, feeling optimistic and happy and ready.

You are ready to let go of the illusions you once thought were real. You are ready to ditch the Illusions Of Commerce, so you can be free of assumptions that stop you from shopping.

You're in the right place. You're here at the perfect time. The ocean is ready to take your illusion and recycle their meaning. All you have to do is let go.

Take another slow deep breath and say to yourself, "I am ready to let go of the Illusions Of Commerce that are confusing me and stopping me from shopping for a man."

***Think about the first Illusion Of Commerce:***
***There aren't enough men to go around.***

Picture the words written on a scrap of paper. There aren't enough men to go around. Look at the scrap of paper in your hand. See how this makes you feel. You're not happy. You feel the scarcity and it's not empowering.

Take another breath and say to yourself, "I let go of this illusion, belief and feeling that there aren't enough men to go around."

Throw the scrap of paper into the ocean. Watch the waves carry it away. Your scrap, and the confusion that this illusion created for you, now dissolves into the ocean. The paper transforms into fish food. You are clear. You know this isn't true. The Illusion: "There aren't enough men to go around" has no power in your life.

### *Think about the second Illusion Of Commerce:*
### *There are no good men left.*

Picture the words written on a scrap of paper. **There are no good men left.** Look at the scrap of paper in your hand. See how this makes you feel. You're not happy. You feel the scarcity and it's not empowering. You can feel the compromise that this illusion suggests and you can see that this is just not true.

Take another breath and say to yourself, "I let go of this illusion, belief and feeling that there are no good men left."

Throw the scrap of paper into the ocean. Watch the waves carry it away. Your scrap and the confusion that this illusion created for you, now dissolves into the ocean. The paper transforms into fish food. You are clear. You know this isn't true. The Illusion, "There are no good men left" has no power in your life.

### *Think about the third Illusion Of Commerce:*
### *You have to lower your standards to have a great relationship.*

Picture the words written on a scrap of paper. **You have to lower your standards to have a great relationship.** Look at the scrap of paper in your hand. See how this makes you feel. It's kind of depressing. You can't be yourself and have high standards or you'll be alone. This is not empowering. You can feel the futility that this illusion suggests. It makes you feel pessimistic and hopeless. You can see that this is just not true.

Take another breath and say to yourself, "I let go of this illusion, belief and feeling that you have to lower your standards to have a great relationship."

Throw the scrap of paper into the ocean. Watch the waves carry it away. Your scrap and the confusion that this illusion created for you, now dissolves into the ocean. The paper transforms into fish food. You are clear. You know this isn't true. The Illusion, "You have to lower your standards to have a great relationship" has no power in your life.

***Think about the fourth Illusion Of Commerce:***
***They look good at first, but then they change.***

Picture the words written on a scrap of paper. **They look good at first, but then they change.** Look at the scrap of paper in your hand. See how this makes you feel. It's annoying. You can't know whom you're dating, because this guy will change into someone else, someone not as caring, loving, faithful and attentive. If he's going to change, then what's the point? This illusion makes you feel discouraged. You can see that this is just not true. It is an illusion of commerce.

Take another breath and say to yourself, "I let go of this illusion, belief and feeling that they look good at first, but then they change."

Throw the scrap of paper into the ocean. Watch the waves carry it away. Your scrap and the confusion that this illusion created for you, now dissolves into the ocean. The paper transforms into fish food. You are clear. You know this isn't true. The Illusion: "They look good at first, but then they change" has no power in your life.

***Think about the fifth Illusion Of Commerce:***
***I can change him and make it work.***

Picture the words written on a scrap of paper. **I can change him and make it work.** Look at the scrap of paper in your hand. See how this makes you feel. Yikes. You already know there are things about this guy that you don't like or that just don't fit with you. If you have to change him and make it work, is he really the guy you want? This illusion makes you feel like dating and love is a project, a fixer-upper. You can see that this is just not true. It is an illusion of commerce.

Take another breath and say to yourself, "I let go of this illusion, belief and feeling that I can change him and make it work."

Throw the scrap of paper into the ocean. Watch the waves carry it away. Your scrap and the deception that this illusion created for you, now dissolves into the ocean. The paper transforms into fish food. You are clear. You know this isn't true. The Illusion: "I can change him and make it work" has no power in your life.

*Think about the sixth Illusion Of Commerce:*
*If he loves me enough, everything will turn out fine.*

Picture the words written on a scrap of paper. **If he loves me enough, everything will turn out fine.** Look at the scrap of paper in your hand. See how this makes you feel. What is enough? When will you know there's enough love? This illusion makes you feel anxious and sad. If he doesn't love you enough now, what does that mean for your relationship? You want everything to be fine, right away, not in some distant future when he loves you enough. You can see that this is just not true. It is an illusion of commerce.

Take another breath and say to yourself, "I let go of this illusion, belief and feeling that if he loves me enough, everything will turn out fine."

Throw the scrap of paper into the ocean. Watch the waves carry it away. Your scrap and the deception that this illusion created for you, now dissolves into the ocean. The paper transforms into fish food. You are clear. You know this isn't true. The Illusion, "If he loves me enough, everything will turn out fine" has no power in your life.

Now take another slow, deep breath.

Look at the ocean and the waves. You have cast away the **Six Illusions Of Commerce** and you are clear. These illusions have no truth. They are just misconceptions. Now, they have no meaning for you. They have no truth. They have no hold on your thinking, your feelings and your actions.

You are free and open to see dating and life in a new, positive and empowering way.

Perfect. Just relax and when you are ready, regroup your energy. Congratulations. You are free of the **Six Illusions Of Commerce** and now you can see dating in a whole new light.

Now smile.

Picture yourself on that gorgeous beach. You can date and find great guys and you are ready to learn how to go shopping for a man.

## Affirmation and Intention:
# POSITIVE POSSIBILITIES IN DATING

Use this affirmation whenever you like to support your new understanding and positive energy and outlook. Try it right now and feel your new strength, freedom and open-minded perspective.

Take a slow deep breath.
Smile and say,

*"I can see the new possibilities in me and in dating."*

CHAPTER

3

# CLEANING THE CLOSETS
## The TOSS, HOLD, KEEP System

After busting up the illusions, it's time to delve into the closet. The closet is where you have all of your clothes. Some of them are up to date and enrich your life. Some of them are worn out, unflattering and basically unwearable. Now, you can examine and eliminate all those clothes that have outlived their use. These clothes that have outlived their usefulness are your notions and thoughts about relationships. They hang in the back of the closet, behind most of the clothes you normally wear. You tucked them away in the recesses of the attic, in dark, dusty boxes. Clean out the closet. Make room for the things you really want. Look at which outfits still fit well and are up to date. Check out which have passed their prime.

The back of your closet holds the obsolete ideas you bought in your youth. These are notions, thoughts, and little titbits of information you crammed into your brain when you were figuring out men. You gather these ideas throughout life. You collect them from conversations. You listen to television and read about all kinds of relationships and add them to your wardrobe of notions. You compile all sorts of information from your family. Each person has notions and they pass them on to you. You graciously accumulate all these ideas throughout life. You amass so much information that you put it away to examine later some time. You don't look at any of them carefully; after all, there is plenty of room in the attic of your mind.

These notions are hand-me-down criteria for romance and love. They remain tucked into the corners of the closet. These thoughts lie hidden in boxes stored on the top shelf. Few people want to get into the closet and look at everything stored there. It seems like work. It takes too long. There are many excuses, but if you don't clean it out, there's no room for more. You end up cramming more things into a tiny space, filled with a lot of useless, outdated clothes. You keep trying to add better quality outfits to your wardrobe, but the armoire is jammed with stuff, some of which you can't even remember buying or getting.

The ideas that you hold about relationships, love and men, are the clothes in your closet. Some of them are clean, stylish and make you feel great. Some of them are definitely past their glory days and need to go. Look at these thoughts and decide which ones work for you and which don't. Put your hands on the blazer that was always too big, but you just couldn't toss. Grab the silk shirt that has a stain, but you might wear it under a sweater, if you find one to match. The old shoes, the plastic belts, the worn out peasant dresses, are all thoughts hiding in the recesses of your beliefs.

This is fun. This is freedom. You can let go of anything that doesn't complement you. Imagine a spacious and bright closet filled with gorgeous clothes. You can have everything you want. There are no limits. Everything fits you perfectly. Each accessory complements your wardrobe. Everything goes together and you feel wonderful.

Every outfit in your closet is an idea about love. Some of them don't enhance your life. Some of these notions limit your freedom. If you clean out your closet, you open yourself for more. You can make room for exciting ideas and possibilities when you let go of some things that just don't work anymore. You can discover new ways of looking at old ideas and see if they merit an update. You can explore fresh thoughts and bring more joy and happiness into your life.

# TOSS. HOLD. KEEP.

Repeat, "Toss. Hold. Keep." in your mind as you delve into the corners of your thoughts and sweep away the cobwebs. Toss the beliefs you swallowed without even noticing. These are ideas about men and love that you took in without thinking, and they don't work for you. Hold the ideas that you haven't examined yet. There is something there, in this notion, that seems right, but you aren't clear about it yet. Keep those tried, true and accurate feelings about partnership. These are your core pieces, the foundations or classics that make a strong and versatile wardrobe. You build your relationship wardrobe around these.

Your closet is the storage depot for everything, whether you need it or not. Now, you can jump right in and clear out the debris. You can look at everything you tucked away and really see whether it brings you joy.

***Toss. Hold. Keep.***
***That's the closet-cleaning mantra.***

## TOSS

Get rid of everything that limits who you are and what you need. You want space, room to grow in a relationship. You gain the freedom to express who you are by letting go of your beliefs and fear about love, men and relationships. Get rid of anything that has holes and stains. Chuck everything that does not fit. Dump the faded, tired, worn out ideas. Examine everything. Throw out anything and everything that doesn't work.

Some of these ideas and beliefs are from childhood. Are you waiting for a man who will take control of everything, someone who will rescue you from the tedium of life? Are you looking for the ruler of the roost? Does a perfect relationship start to look like the fairy tales you read or the television programs of your youth? Did you buy a fantasy of what works and then try to fit into it?

Everyone buys ideas and dreams about relationships. As a five year old, your ideal man may have been your father or an uncle. He could have been Sir Galahad or Romeo. Whatever he did or however he behaved, he was a model for your ideal man. You based a notion of what a good man is, on whom you encountered. You saw things. You picked up ideas and imagined how it would be for you with a man like this.

Later, it may have been a teacher, whose gentle but firm command of the classroom became the symbol of the only man for you. In teen years, the guy who had the great car, or poetic nature or the bad guy or the captain of the basketball team was the perfect catch. All of these ideas are looming in the back of your closet, forming a thick layer of dust on your next romance.

What do you think a perfect man is? Why do you think that? Did you have a turbulent home life where everyone yelled at each other? Are you still holding onto this idea of a relationship, as though it's the way life is? Maybe you think that all married people fight and fight often. Maybe you think that all men are loud and angry. Maybe you think that women have to scream to get their way. Start to notice what you think about this, if you had a loud family life.

Were your parents very quiet? Do you think that having a quiet home life is the perfect example of harmony in a partnership? Maybe men with strong opinions bother you. You may feel uncomfortable arguing your point of view because your idea about a good relationship is one where everyone agrees.

Did you come from a single parent family? Did you hear conversations about how bad men are? Maybe you think that men leave anyway. You might think that because your father left the family, all men will leave and hurt you. Maybe you have this quietly painful idea about men and love because that's what you saw or heard.

*"Your closet needs to be a place of joy and celebration of who are you now - not who you were."*
*Stacy London*

It's a great feeling to realize that some thoughts outlive their use. You don't need them any more. They don't give you happiness. They don't empower you. They don't help you get what you want. Most of these thoughts are covered with other thoughts. They may all sound true, but they're not. They are just thoughts. You don't need any thought that gets in the way of love.

Look at the images you bought about relationships and you will discover many socks that do not match and a lot of pantyhose with runs. The key to finding the badlands of your closet is to look for the biggest complaints you have about love, men and relationships.

What do you really complain about with men?
Why do you think men are like that?
What do men do that really bothers you?
Where did you get that idea?
What things don't measure up to the ideas you hold?

Try this Belief Exercise to discover some of your ongoing complaints and beliefs about men and love. Grab some paper or something to take real notes and fill in the blanks in the rest of the sentences in the Belief Exercise. Have some fun with it and be honest.

At the end of this chapter there is a section for this Belief Exercise so you can have more time and more room to discover the ideas and beliefs you have about guys and dating that limit. You can go back to it anytime and fill in more beliefs that you don't see right now.

## Belief Exercise

Every time I fall in love I end up ...
None of my relationships really worked out because
I hate it when I finally fall in love and then ...
Why does love have to be so ...
Every time I meet a man he ends up ...
I can't understand why men always ...
I can't believe that men think ...
I hate it when men ...
Men always ...
Men never ...
Relationships are never ...
First there is so much love and then ...
Why don't men ...
I hate it when men act ...
Why are all the men I meet ...
I need a man who ...
The best men are the ones who ...
I really thought he was great because he ...
All men ...
My ideal man is ... because he ...

Any of the answers you gave are complaints. If every time you find a man who has X, and then you find out it is really Z, you found a complaint. If you discover that every time you find a man you think is right for you and then he turns out to be married, stupid, uncaring, unwilling to commit, etc., then you found one of your complaints. There are hundreds of complaints. Once you train your ear to hear them and your mind to listen for them, you can loosen their hold on you. You can see what your complaints are and whether they bring you any joy or love.

Underneath these complaints lie the ideas you hold about them. You have an idea. If you feel it's true, then you complain about it. If you complain that all men cheat on their wives, then you have the idea that all men cheat. Is this going to help you find a terrific life partner? No. Why? You think all men cheat. You will find that evidence and know it's true. You might settle for a man, knowing he will cheat on you sometimes. You may decide not to be with a man because you think, eventually, he will cheat on you.

This thought limits your joy. How can you be happy shopping, dating and looking for a great guy, if you know that whomever you choose is going to hurt you later? The complaints can't give you any freedom. How can you enjoy dressing up if you know that you're stuck with worn out clothes in your closet? This is the TOSS pile. Toss out the worn out, misguided, unflattering ideas and your closet has more room for a great wardrobe.

Make room for a new relationship and a great guy. Now, you have space in your closet for a man who is faithful, loving, fun and more. A great wardrobe needs a clear vision and a great space. Everything fits and it's all in perfect condition. So anything that doesn't bring you joy, fulfilment and real partnership goes into the Toss pile.

## HOLD

The Hold pile is the maybe stuff. It has the sweatshirt you wear twice a year to clean the garage and the seventh in a line of white shirts. The Hold pile contains the jeans that are just a tad too small, but you can fit into them as long as you don't eat. It contains the high-heeled shoes that you can wear if you are going to be sitting, not standing. You're just not sure whether you can get rid of them quite yet.

The Hold pile is still on the toss list, but it hasn't reached the trash yet. You want to look at these items and see if there is anything in them worth saving. There may be something to them. Even outdated clothes and accessories may have a value to you. Just wait. You may cast them off soon, but not just yet.

Your Hold pile harbours your notions of comfort, not your early beliefs and core issues. These notions annoy you. They limit you, but it's a quiet, nagging feeling. They may really be part of your Toss list. You just can't see that yet.

In this pile you have a pair of black, snakeskin pumps. You bought them to complement that incredible scarlet dress that stretches to fit every curve. Those shoes look fabulous with your red dress. The problem is that the shoes don't fit well. Every time you wear them, which isn't very often, they hurt your feet. Yes, they're in great condition. So what! They hurt your feet. You legs get tired and your feet swell up after just an hour in these great pumps. You hardly wear the red dress, which is stunning, because those shoes need to go.

Sometimes it's hard to be objective. You can't decide which action to take. Just like these shoes, the idea seemed right at the time, but something is really off now. It doesn't quite work. You may know what it is, and rationalize it away. You may have no clue. It just seems iffy. This is the Hold pile. You'll toss them out, but not just yet.

The Hold pile contains more subtle ideas about men and relationships. These ideas and assumptions don't come blaring across the loud speakers in your mind. They pick at you in little mosquito sounds that just irritate.

What if you think men don't understand women? This is a very annoying idea, because you want a man in your life. It may not make you head for the hills and stay away from all men, but it doesn't make looking for a man very much fun. You know that deep inside no man will understand you. These may be those black snakeskin pumps. You know they pinch, but you can't throw them out yet. If you have ideas that toss around in your mind like this one, take the time to notice them. See how many times this idea or assumption pops into your head. It isn't a thought that will give you joy. It limits your ability to get what you want, because you want a partner who understands you. Keep it in the Hold box until you can examine it more closely.

Some of your ideas are really sound, but they need a little work. You need to update them. The black, wool crepe skirt in the cedar closet would go so well with your beige cashmere sweater. It could do with shortening and some tailoring. You bought it when you were ten pounds heavier. Now it sits in limbo. It's in the Hold pile.

What idea could a black, crepe skirt represent? You want a strong man who can weather the storms life tends to throw. This idea is a good one, generally. It's your idea about what a strong man is that needs work. Strong is good. Domineering and controlling is not. When you were young, strong men had authority. They ordered you around and you did what they said. They had the final say in everything. It didn't matter what you thought was right when you were five. You weren't in a position to have equality at that age. That strong man knew much better than you did. He made you feel safe. Maybe you kept that idea of strong from your childhood. It doesn't work now. You're older. The quality of strength means something different. You haven't examined this idea in a long time, and there is something a little off with how it looks. Hold the black, crepe skirt for now. Then, take it to a good tailor. Alter it to fit you well. You've grown up. A strong man looks a lot better with some alterations in your perceptions. Now a strong man is "count-on-able." He gives good feedback. He doesn't dominate. He has your back. He has his own opinions and respects you for your opinions, too. He appreciates you.

What about those sterling silver earrings you have? They've been sitting in your jewelry box, because one of the backs is too loose. They look great and are perfect for you, but they need some work. Put them into the Hold pile. Look at them. These earrings may reflect the story you read where the two people succeeded against all odds and made life work for them. They had hardships and life was against them, but they overcame it all. This may not be the ideal you want to create in your relationship. It isn't your real truth, but you may choose situations, create circumstances or even judge men by this ideal, because this thought is bouncing around your brain.

Fixing the backs of the earrings updates the fantasy that you have to surmount terrible things to have a great relationship. Life can bring ups and downs but, in this idea, you struggle against life. Have the jeweler fix the earrings. You want to alter this thought so that when you meet someone he can help you to meet the challenges of life, not create life as a struggle against everything and everyone. The earrings, the ideas, may be keepers, but they need a little work.

## KEEP

These are the true feelings that hold your ideas of relationship solid. The Keep pile is definitely the basis for your sparkling wardrobe. These are qualities and perceptions that bring you joy and strength. These are the ideas that work for you. When you think about this idea about men or love, you feel good and you know that's what you want.

Monogamy is a classic idea for our recent times. Does this work for you? Do you want one man who will be there for you, through thick and thin? Do you want one man in your life? Do you picture yourself with the same man, faithful to the end, in love to your final days? Yes? This idea is your 14 Karat gold bangle bracelet. It has value, worth and will last forever. You wear it all the time and still get compliments. This idea will stand the test of time and keep you happy. You know that life with one great man will bring you joy, freedom and enhance your life. This bracelet is a good, beautiful, dependable staple in your wardrobe of ideas. Keep it in your special jewelry box, knowing this is a treasure.

*"The best way to choose what to keep and what to throw away is to take each item in one's hand and ask: "Does this spark joy?"*
*If it does, keep it. If not, dispose of it."*
*Marie Kondo*

The Keep pile is the easiest to spot. When you enter your closet, you know which items you wear all of the time. You know which ones fit well. You know which ones bring compliments. You know which styles and colors suit you well and spice up your life. It's the same with your ideas about men and relationships. You know which ideas work for you. These can be thoughts about the beauty of love, the experience of sharing life with a remarkable man. These thoughts give you strength and joy. These are the keepers.

Your Keep pile contains the staples of your wardrobe and your best feelings, ideas and criteria about men. These are the classics that will really work for you. These are your best black slacks, your gorgeous pumps, the blouse that always looks amazing and that fabulous gold necklace that always brings compliments. Put them in the front of the closet. If the shoe fits, keep it. Wear it with style and get some great accessories, too! Don't worry, if you need more staples, you can always go shopping. I'm going to show you how to shop.

# HAVING FUN IN
# THE CLOSET OF BAD IDEAS

It can be hilarious to find out what you really think about men and love. Most of these ideas have no truth. You picked them up in your first conversations about sex. Remember when you were very young and you asked someone about sex? Their ideas were just a bit left of the truth. Maybe you were five, and asked a very experienced seven year old all about sex. Well, you got a very creative answer, based on what this older friend knew, heard and imagined. Was it the truth? Not. Even if it was close, you pictured something very different from the real thing. The same thing applies to your thoughts about men and relationships. All through life, you heard things, imagined things and then assumed they were true. It's time to shake those boxes in storage and make room for some fashion flair.

*Stop living in the closet of bad ideas.*

If you want to really laugh, get a group of gals together and ask them to answer the questions at the beginning of this section. Have each one fill in the blanks. Then, read them out loud. You will probably agree with half of them. The others you will find really amusing. As you go through the list of complaints, you'll see what you think men are really like. It's awful. It's also very funny. None of the notions are true, but they sure sound like the truth. No wonder women have such a hard time. They think all of this about men. Have a good laugh. The best way to see which bathing suits flatter you the most is to try on plenty that make you look awful. Don't be upset. Laugh. Some of those bathing suits are absurd. Then you can try on some wonderful new suits and make a shopping splash.

Issues of style are always important. Style is what works, what complements your goals and your lifestyle. You want to look into your life and see what satisfies you. The dream lover your best friend wants may never be your type of man. If you like to live on the edge and you thrive with the excitement in your life, someone else's ideal man who is calm and reserved may not suit you. Your mother's choice and ideas may not fulfill you. Society's concoction of what a perfect relationship is may not be true for you. This is a matter of style, personality and preference. You are shopping for exactly what you want. You have to know what doesn't work, what may be ready for updating and what has to be there no matter what.

Are you ready to accept the minor flaws in a person as well as the virtues? Are you willing to love this man with all of his good and bad points firmly intact? If you are, then you have a wide, sterling silver bracelet that you can wear with nearly every outfit. Keep everything that really works for you. The great black leather boots; the embroidered, antique, silk shawl; and the taupe trench coat complement your life and are in perfect condition. Keep the well-made classics that never go out of style.

vAcceptance has nothing to do with changing the deficiencies, redeeming the person, or lowering your standards. That's all covered in the section on illusions. A minor flaw is a quirky trait. It is something you can get used to, like his having to watch every sport event. These minor flaws are all things you can have in your world and really not worry about. These are just quirks. You have them too.

## Controversial Statement

Some goods are fatally flawed. Beware of major damage and major defects. Major damage is defective material. Lying, cheating, stealing, any kind of abuse and disrespect are major defects. Accepting any of these hurts you. Dump these items/men immediately.

*No amount of tailoring, cleaning or attention is going to turn a moth eaten dress into a stunning outfit.*

There are men who have deep-rooted problems that no one should accept. If any one of them ever threatens you, harms you or berates you, throw them out at once. Don't look back. Don't examine them for other good qualities. It doesn't matter whether a ripped blouse has good buttons on it. Get rid of it at once.

Abuse is a deliberate assault. It can be emotional or physical, either way, you get hurt. A man must respect, love and honor you in the fullest sense. If not, he doesn't deserve to have you in his life. Picture a man who really loves his car. It's a 1964 Corvette Stingray. He takes great care of it. He pampers it with the best products and service. He even dotes on it. Do you think he would drive it into a tree and smash it up, just because he was angry? No, he wouldn't. He loves his car. He would never intentionally damage it. He would never pour cheap oil into the engine or scratch up the fine leather interior. Well, how can a car be more important than a person? Is your life worth less than metal and a motor? You are an amazing creation. You are a fabulous person. Never think that a man who loves you has any right or any excuse to harm you. There is something terribly wrong and twisted with him. This guy is a Toss.

If you know a man who is an abuser, tell every woman about him. Warn them. These women are your sisters. Do you want your sister, your daughter, your mother, your aunt to be threatened or abused? These men should be wearing signs that say, "I beat women and I abuse women emotionally. I hate women. I am a hurtful idiot." You need these signs, because many women don't know how to see abuse. It doesn't matter if you don't feel worthy. No matter what, you do not deserve to be abused and you do not have to accept abuse in any form. There are absolutely no excuses for this behavior. None.

You know that if a store treats you badly, that if it doesn't honor their sales or sells really inferior products, you will never go back to that store again. You'll also tell all your friends about it, too. Of course! Why would you go there again and have a bad experience? Why would you let your friends go there? You'll tell them that store is bad, don't shop there.

This handsome man-package who treats you badly may look good for a little while, but he is really a deadly virus. Don't ever bring him into your home or your life. Don't think you can change him with love or understanding. You can't. Send him away at the very first hint of problems.

Put a sign on him that says, "Plague! Enter into this relationship at your own risk." He's an Ebola boy. Off to the dumpster without hesitation.

Women have the key to something very special. They are the holders of society. In the other animal groups, the female chooses her mate for very specific reasons. She chooses the strong, vital male who will protect, provide and join with her to produce healthy children. Even though you have many more criteria for a life long relationship, your choice of partner creates and holds our society. If a guy doesn't treat you right, then he isn't a quality guy. Do you want to reward this horrible behavior by loving a man like this? Do you want to bring more abusive, destructive people into the world? You have a choice. At the first sign of harsh treatment, toss him out. Don't date him. Don't move in with him. Don't have his children. Don't accept mistreatment. Put those moth-eaten garments into the trash at once! Yes. I know I sound strong and adamant. I am. I am your shopping advocate so you can have the best dating experiences and relationships. You are an amazing gal. You deserve to be loved, treated well and respected. That's all.

There are wonderful, honest loving men out there just waiting to share your life. I know there are. Many of my guy clients ask me about finding fabulous women in their lives. They are really out there and ready for a great relationship. You are a very precious gift. You are an amazing, dynamic woman. You can have a great man and a rewarding relationship. You are out in the "Great Galactic Shopping Mall Of Love" looking for a man to share the beauty of life with you. Shop wisely.

*"Someone you haven't met yet is already dreaming of adoring you."*
*Danielle LaPorte*

# Visualization and Affirmation
# CLEANING THE CLOSETS

Now that you understand the Toss, Hold, Keep System, you can do the next visualization and affirmation to Toss the ideas and beliefs that limit your shopping success. Here is the new visualization to clear the debris in your closet. After all, if you can't fit the clothes in your closet, then you are cramping your own style.

Start with the "3 Steps To Centering" exercise and then go to the **Cleaning The Closets Visualization**. Grab the piece of paper you used to finish the sentences in the Belief Exercise.

## Visualization:
## Cleaning The Closets

Take a deep breath.

Picture yourself in your bedroom. This can be an imaginary room or your real bedroom.

You're ready to clean your closet and make room for great new clothes, shoes, purses and accessories. You are ready to get rid of things that no longer serve you, are out of style or that just don't do it for you anymore. In other words, you are ready to let go of the beliefs that clutter you mind and heart, as well as your closet. You have all of your clothes in piles, ready to sort. You have large boxes and garbage bags ready, so you can simply get rid of the ideas and beliefs that don't work. Some ideas are just not flattering. Others are really worn out. They have no shine. The clothes that you see right now represent the beliefs and ideas that just don't work any more. These are the items on your list from the TOSS Pile exercise.

Once you see all of those piles, you can imagine what your closet will look like. It's clean. Everything is organized. You know once your closet is in order, you'll have more energy, more clarity and much more fun. Who wants to get stuck in the closet with old worn out clothes that don't even suit you anymore? Not you. All you have to do is let go and Toss them.

Take another slow deep breath and say to yourself, "I am ready toss the ideas and beliefs that do not serve me, benefit me or empower me."

Think about all of the beliefs, ideas and conversations about men and dating that no longer serve and empower you. Take your list from the Belief Exercise. Choose the first idea and belief from your list.

Take another breath, read the first belief.
Then say to yourself, "I Toss this belief and idea into the trash. This is not true, and it doesn't empower me. Into the garbage you go."

Go through the beliefs and say the declaration after you read each one. When you finish, take a slow deep breathe and say, "These beliefs are gone. I am free to see the truth and have more fun dating."

Congratulations. You learned the TOSS. HOLD. KEEP. System of Cleaning The Closets. You can use this system again and again to see if you have other ideas about guys and dating that don't serve or empower you. Now you'll see yourself and dating in a whole new light.

Now, smile.
Your closet is clean and now you have room to go shopping for a man. You just made room for a fabulous guy to enter your life!

## Affirmation and Intention:
## CLEARING THE WAY

Use this affirmation to increase support for your positive energy and outlook about dating. Try it right now and feel your new strength, freedom and open-minded perspective.

Take a slow deep breath.
Smile and say,

"I let go of the beliefs that no longer serve me.
***I clear the way for a great relationship.***"

Are you feeling ready to go shopping for a man?
Fabulous. Now, you need a really great shopping list.

## Belief Exercise

Take a few deep breaths and just finish these sentences. You can start with the "3 Steps To Centering" exercise to help you get in a clear mind space.

And have fun. Some of your beliefs are hilarious.

Every time I fall in love I end up …

None of my relationships really worked out because …

I hate it when I finally fall in love and then …

Why does love have to be so …

Every time I meet a man he ends up …

I can't understand why men always …

I can't believe that men think ...

I hate it when men ...

Men always ...

Men never ...

Relationships are never ...

First there is so much love and then ...

Why don't men ...

I hate it when men act …

Why are all the men I meet …

I need a man who …

The best men are the ones who …

I really thought he was great because he …

All men …

My ideal man is … because he …

# Cleaning The Closets Notes & Insights

# THE CONSUMMATE CONSUMER

## Creating Your Shopping for a Man List

Shattering illusions is a lot of fun. Cleaning out your closet opens up a world of possibilities to try on. When you realize what you think is not necessarily the truth, you have a lot of room for play. This is great. You are starting to get ready to shop. Do you have your list?

What no list? A list is crucial to really get what you want. How many times have you gone to the supermarket without a list and forgotten the milk or butter or bread? You walk into the store and head down the first aisle. There is a rambling conversation in your mind.

"Gee, the fresh fruit looks fabulous today. The cantaloupes are on sale and they smell so sweet. All right, I'll just throw one in the cart. I already have a head of lettuce, but this is Romaine, and it would go well with some sun-dried tomatoes. I have balsamic vinegar at home, so that will be great."

You turn the cart and continue. "I don't need any meats today, but that chicken breast looks delicious." Into the cart it goes. Further down the aisle is a little cooking display. Strong spices and a touch of garlic start to make you salivate. A friendly looking woman prepares stir-fried veggies with fresh pea pods, asparagus tips, red peppers and cashews. The closer you get, the better it smells. Naturally, you run back to the vegetable aisle and pop the rest of the ingredients into your cart.

You decide to avoid the pastry aisle. Wise choice, but there is a display of fresh biscotti at the corner of the cereal aisle. It is strategically placed where you have to pick up some granola. You get hooked again. You do manage to pick up the milk, butter and half and half. Finally, you are in the last section, and whip straight through to the check-out counter. Now, you look into your cart. As you take every item and put it on the belt, you are a little surprised at how much is there, but you know you'll eat it all anyway. The cashier gives you the total. It's definitely more than you expected to pay, but it'll be worth it.

Then, you get everything home. You unpack the bags and start to put all of this marvelous food into the refrigerator. You forgot that you already have some chicken in the meat bin. So, you rationalize that you'll freeze it, or have chicken twice this week. Dairy products are fine, and you really did need these. The vegetables are another story. Too many, and you have a full head of lettuce and some broccoli, peppers, scallions, and spinach that you forgot. So, all of that great stuff for the stir fry is beyond what you can eat in a week. That's all right. You'll invite some friends over for dinner. Casual. Just girls night in.

Checking your dates on the calendar, you realize you already have plans to go out to dinner on Wednesday night. There's a business lunch on Thursday, and you never eat much after that. Work-out at the gym on Friday is always late, and you usually connect with some people and have a little bite at the restaurant near-by. Saturday you have a date with someone for dinner and a movie.

Oh well, you'll figure something out. Biscotti in hand you go to the pantry, where another box of little cookies stares you in the face. You bought those to go with your morning coffee, too. Coffee! You forgot the coffee. You shake the container and console yourself that at least you have enough for tomorrow morning.

Does this sound vaguely familiar? The beautiful displays, the goods on sale, the smells and music will confuse you. The company designed them to attract your attention. Remember, it's shopping. Without a list you'll get distracted. You'll end up not getting what you set out for. You bring home something you hadn't planned for and didn't really want and are probably spending much more time and money than anticipated.

---

*Make your list and check it twice.*
*Dating's not gambling or rolling the dice.*

Shopping for a man is no different. Those deep-set eyes, that tight butt, the way his lip quivers when he is thinking. Looks very appealing. You met him in the health club and he seems so dashing. He works out and looks great. He likes to laugh, and he carries a brief case, so he must do well financially. He tantalizes your senses and you put him in your shopping cart without even considering what you are going to do with him later on. Great display. Perfect lighting. Buy me. Buy me.

Unless you want a one-night plaything, you have no list. You have not pragmatically considered what you are shopping for in a partner. In the past month, this man dated at least ten of the women in the club. The gossip is not particularly flattering, but he sure does look good. You're lonely, and it's been a while since someone in this neat package has delighted your libido. Great. If what you want is this particular tango, go for it. Just don't have any expectations that the tango will go on for more than a dance.

To be a consummate consumer you need a list. This list has all the attributes in a partner that you need and want. This is going to be very pragmatic, and there is a lot to consider. This is not a superficial outer appearance kind of description. It has nothing to do with tall, dark and handsome or light, thin and good looking. These are the fundamental qualities that you want in a partner. This is definitely hardcore.

Terry, a client of mine, was continually finding guys that really didn't suit her. Beautiful, accomplished and attractive, she was focused on going with the flow. Unfortunately, things were not flowing in her direction. It wasn't that she couldn't find guys to date, it was that she found the wrong guys to date. They just didn't have the same goals, focus or standards. I was working with her as her life coach and this included helping her with her *Shopping For A Man* list. It was slow going. The list made her feel limited.

I wanted her to have fun, and to keep a playful image in her mind. I asked her what size shoe she wore. "Size eight," she said. "Why?" So I asked, "Why are you shopping for a size 6 shoe, when you know you need a size 8?" There was silence on the line for a moment and then she started laughing. "Are you saying that all the guys I'm dating are a size 6?" "Yes," I said. "And not only that, they are cramping your toes and making you limp." She laughed even more, and then said, "I need some new shoes. I'm going shopping."

Since then, the secret code for dating with her gal pals is "Let's go Shoe Shopping."

Your Shopping List is more about you than it is about the guy. This is a beautiful and fun exploration of what is really important to you in life. Your Shopping List is where you come face to face with who you are, what you need and what you want. You are creating a list of the qualities you admire and need in a guy and those qualities you admire and strive for in yourself. The qualities and attributes on your list are qualities that you have and that you respect. What you write on the list shows how you live your life. That's powerful and insightful. It helps you understand yourself. Knowing who you are, what you really admire and strive for, how you live your life from the inside out, is key to loving yourself and finding a quality guy who will love that about you, too. It's also a pathway to personal growth. This is not a wish list. Yes, you are focusing on his qualities, but the process is one of self-discovery.

If you wear a size ten dress, you need to know it. There's no sense in trying on a size seven or a size fourteen. You're a size ten, so when you go shopping that's the rack to check out. There may be hundreds of gorgeous clothes in size five. There may be some very fabulous things in the Big Women's department, but you are never going to come home with anything worthwhile if you purchase an outfit there. It's not going to fit well. You are not going to enjoy it, use it, and feel fantastic every time you slip into that number. A true assessment of what you need will give you the opportunity to get it.

Examine what you really need. If you are looking for a man who loves you deeply and is going to be there through good times and bad, then put this on your list. This man is a well-made, well-tailored, wool coat. It is perfect for you. It's warm, fits well and has plenty of room for a suit or sweater underneath. It will stand the test of fashion fads, through many good years of flattering, impeccable wear. It will keep you warm and dry when the weather gets harsh. It will always make sure that everything inside is clean, in good shape and well protected. Don't stop at the nylon sweat-suit section. The great coat is not there, it isn't what you want, and it will never last.

*"After assessing what's in your closet, make a list of what you need. Not want, but need. Whatever the blank spots, write them down. This will be your reference for shopping."*
*Nina Garcia*

# THE 7 CRUCIAL ITEMS ON YOUR SHOPPING LIST

Creating your list is an ongoing process. You'll discover a great deal about what you need in your life and where you've been fooling yourself. Take plenty of time. This is your real shopping list for your man and will reveal so many things that you will uncover. You may find you need something on your list, you forgot something major on your list or you have lots of things to delete. This list could take you a month of work, and you will still notice new things and update your thoughts.

*If it's not on the list, then it doesn't exist.*

*There are specific qualities that I recommend putting on every list you make.*

## NUMBER ONE: He's available.

It has to be on the market shelf, ready for purchase. There's absolutely no sense in shopping otherwise. Available means that he is unattached. He has no commitments to anyone else. Someone who is available is open to sharing his life with a wonderful woman. He is looking for a solid, committed relationship. He is an open, loving man. He listens to you and considers what you say to be valuable. He is available. He is open emotionally and personally. He is ready to have a relationship, so he makes time for you and invites you to participate in his life. Anything less, and you don't have a remote chance for harmony and joy.

When you are shopping in the world you are looking for something that is for sale. You don't usually go into the store and ask the sales person if you can buy the store's lighting fixtures. They belong to the store. They aren't for sale. Don't ask to buy the display.

When you are shopping, you don't look for anything that isn't available. So first, unavailable means already committed, not interested in a committed relationship and not on the market. A married man is in a committed relationship. He is the display. It doesn't matter whether it's quality merchandise. It's not available.

What's great about this, about making sure he's available, is that you will have no considerations, no hesitations, no blocks and no worries that there is some strange back story, lost love, past relationship, emotional block in his life that will stop the relationship from being the perfect fit. Go to the store to buy what is for sale without any conditions. ***It has to be on the list.***

## NUMBER TWO: He is madly in love with you.

You certainly don't need anyone around who doesn't love and appreciate you. This is big time. You could have everything else in a relationship, but if love is missing, it feels very hollow. So, what do I mean here? You know what love is. He knows what love is. He wants to share his love with you. You want to share your love with him. Remember this is your list and love is a non-negotiable item on this list. The clear understanding of love has to be there. This is a requirement.

Love comes at an appropriate time in a relationship. Love usually develops over time. You get to know and appreciate each other and see it grow. The love and commitment grows stronger every day. Of course people fall in love at first sight. Even in this remarkable situation, growth, understanding and appreciation of each other comes in stages. You still need time to see how you connect and how your lives can come together in joyful, caring, supportive and powerful ways.

Don't fall for the "I love you" ten minutes after you've been together. This means, "I'd love to have sex with you." It does not mean, "I love you and since I am looking for a wife, please stay tuned."

Make sure you have love on your list. This is the most fabulous part of your shopping. This is about shopping for the ring, but it's also about the truth in emotions and a celebration of heart to heart. He loves you. You love him. This will give the relationship joy and beauty.

## NUMBER THREE: He wants this relationship.

This is the quality that helps you know that he made a commitment to you and your relationship together. He may be available and he may love you. If he doesn't want to be there through all of life's situations, then no amount of convincing is going to make him stay. Life throws a variety of challenges and joys into our path. There is no pair of pantyhose that hasn't gotten a snag or two. There is no blouse that didn't get dirty and need cleaning. It's life's dance. Be very clear. You need someone who wants to dance with you and only you. Don't pick someone who is moaning about a lost love and will only make due with you. Don't bother with a man who talks a good game and doesn't follow through. Pick a man who really wants to be with you. Remember, it's all right on the label!

How do you know that he wants to be with you? He pays attention to you. He pays more attention to you than to the stunning woman who just walked by, the sports event on the television over the bar, the last woman that he dated who just happened to be at the party you both attended last night. He doesn't stay at work every night. He wants to come home to you, and he does.

You are so important to him that he makes sure you know it. In little ways, he shows you. These are the actions that tell you. You receive gifts. My personal motto is, "Send Presents." He gives you things that he thinks you would like or need. He saw you struggling when you were peeling the potatoes, so he brought you a small vegetable peeler. He says with a smile, "I don't want you to cut those beautiful hands." He may not wrap this little item, but he was thinking about you and just showed it.

## NUMBER FOUR: He appreciates you.

He thinks you are outstanding. He is proud of you and what you do. He accepts you for who you are. He doesn't need to change you. In his eyes, you are the best thing going and he still knows your weaknesses. A man who appreciates you is going to help you shine in the world. He's going to speak highly of you to others and he's going to tell you how much he appreciates you. He knows how lucky he is to be sharing his life with you. He lets you know it and he shows you in so many different ways. He doesn't do this because you look great, cook well, you laugh at his jokes or you clean the house. He doesn't do this because you have a great business, have powerful friends or make him look good. He knows who you are and this thrills him.

Don't even bother with anyone who doesn't appreciate you. You're not going to teach them how to value you. If he's going to criticize you about every little thing, he doesn't get it. You are a vibrant, wonderful, full and rich woman. If he doesn't see this right away, find someone who does. Don't give your time to someone who continually corrects your behavior. Don't stay with a man who lets you know that you don't live up to his standards, or intentionally puts you down. Get real. Dump him.

There are many times when we need someone to tell us we slipped up. If you accidentally hurt his mother's feelings, you want to know. It's appropriate that he tells you. "Gee, honey, when you told my mother...it really hurt her." This gives you the chance to apologize and make things better again. On the other hand, if he says, "You hurt my mother. You are always hurting someone with that big mouth of yours. Who do you think you are?" He is berating you. He doesn't value you. Give it up and get out. Quick and easy. This dress is ill fitting, poorly made and certainly does not complement you. Don't bother thinking about trying it on.

## NUMBER FIVE: He supports you.

He is there to help you be yourself. That is support. If you are a businesswoman, he listens to your decisions and you know that he is on your side. He will give you advice, not because he needs to stroke his ego, not because he thinks that you have no skill or expertise, but because he wants to help you as much as he can. If you are a mother and a homemaker, he helps you. He helps you raise the children with integrity and love and honors your contribution. This isn't just about chores, but I certainly hope you shop for a guy who does chores, contributes to your life, helps raise your children, and makes your life easier.

When I say he supports you, this doesn't mean you pick someone who always agrees with everything you do. That's boring. You won't learn anything new from him. It's okay if your guy has a different opinion, as long as he honors your opinion, too. He will certainly disagree, but you want him to come from a place in the conversation that gives you choices, insight and empowerment.

Let's say you had a fight with your father. He said something, then you said something and you stormed out of the house in a rage. Your lover apologizes to the family for the uproar and comes after you. He puts his arm around you and listens to what you need to say. You tell him your father always does that and that it always hurts you. He listens, and when you're ready, he tells you he loves you.

He also lets you know that this is the way your father is and nothing you will do is going to change that. He says he knows you love your father. He says he knows you know that you have to love your father the way he is and not the way you want him to be. Then he suggests that you go back to the house and apologize for yelling at him. He didn't tell you that you were wrong. He didn't tell you that you were bad. He didn't ask you to apologize to your father for what you said or felt. He simply suggested that you apologize for yelling and disturbing the family. This is courtesy. He knows that you love your father but that he always pushes your buttons. Later you may have a talk and find a way to communicate with your father. Right now, he's suggesting a quick apology and a quick retreat. All in support of you.

This example shows you a level of support that is not weak or patronizing. You picked a man who sees who you are, sees the situation and tries to come up with the best suggestion to help you. This is support.

## NUMBER SIX: He listens.

When you talk, he listens to what you say. He considers you important. What you tell him is important. Naturally, everyone has lapses in their attention. You have a hard day. You are tired, and just plain cranky. This is understandable. When you have something to say, whether it is about a problem at work, or a decision you are making or you want to talk about the relationship, he is right there. He is attentive. He is considering what you are saying.

Listening is a skill. You have to stop coming up with little anecdotes and comments in your own head and pay attention to what the other person is saying. You want to hear what that person says and how they feel or think, whether you are needed for advice or just to be a loving space for conversation.

One of the biggest complaints women have is that their partner doesn't listen to them. If he doesn't take the time and attention to listen, that's a good clue to how the relationship will unfold. Remember this.

*If a guy doesn't listen to you,*
*this might mean that he doesn't think what you are saying*
*is as important as what he is thinking.*

## NUMBER SEVEN: He is honest.

Very basic. He doesn't lie. He doesn't cheat. He doesn't steal. And he doesn't fudge the truth. He is an honorable man. You know that when he tells you something, whether it's about how he feels, what he thinks or what's going on, he is being open and honest. This means no hidden agendas to manipulate you. This means no ulterior motives. When he says he loves you, it means just that. He doesn't say it so you have sex, or lend him money or agree to something you are not comfortable with or think of him as wonderful and caring when he is not. He means it.

Honesty includes integrity. So you know when he says something or does something, you can count on him. He means it when he says he is too tired to talk. He means it when he says you did a marvelous job. You can count on this person.

If you buy a shirt that says wash and wear and it shreds or shrinks in the machine, you bought a lie. Take it back to the store and demand your money back. Write a letter to the manufacturer. You want an honest representation. If you bought a man that lies or cheats, send him back. Put a new label on him. The manufacturer obviously made a mistake with this one. Remember those illusions? You are not going to change him. You brought home damaged goods. Hurry to your senses and get rid of the merchandise.

The 7 Crucial Items on your Shopping list are non-negotiable parts of your list for a reason. They were on the top of my list. These are the seven aspects, seven qualities that I knew I could never compromise and find a man that would have my back, love me madly and share my life. That's why they're here. They are a powerful foundation.

Once you have the "7 Crucial Items on your Shopping List," you can begin to add your personal preferences. Now come all of those facets of a man and a relationship that are going to make it very clear who you are and what you want. Don't worry about putting every-thing in order of its importance. The objective is to discover what you are really looking for so you can be a Consummate Consumer.

# IT'S ALL ABOUT YOU CREATING A PERSONAL SHOPPING LIST

## Personal Taste and Self Discovery

Physical attraction is a given. You're not going to pick a guy that doesn't attract you. Don't describe his looks or put any limitations on his appearance on your list. If you have a particular racial or religious preference, put that down. Even if he is much taller than you or shorter than you, who he is beneath the looks is what you are buying. This is a pragmatic list. You're looking for the man who has qualities that you want to live with for the rest of your life. It doesn't matter if his hair is curly. In fifteen years he could be bald. It doesn't matter if he has brown eyes and you love blue, as long as those eyes look at you with deep love and joy.

**_Shop smart and carry a big list._**

This is your shopping list. It's a detailed list because you don't want to have to go back to the store with a return. You want to get as close to your ideal as possible and that requires a real, working, detailed list. If you are lazy about writing a great and detailed list, then you may end up with someone who doesn't meet your needs in a man and in a relationship. Your list? Don't leave home without it.

Do you want a man with a sense of humor? Do you want a man who knows how to have fun? Do you want him to have social skills so you can go anywhere with him and enjoy yourself? Do you want him to get along with your family? If these ring a bell with you, write them on the list.

Are you athletic and want a man who can keep up with you? Do you want children? If so, a man who wants a family is going to be on your list. If you have children, you want a man who will love your children and be comfortable with that arrangement. Do you want a man who will take responsibility? He wants to work and help bring in the money. He works hard and enjoys it or at least makes sure he does his part to keep the green coming. He is responsible. Put this on your list.

This is going to be a long list. If you can't come up with at least twenty-five qualities, descriptions and attributes, you're in trouble. This is not about winging it. Your list is about what you want and it's also a process of self-discovery. You will discover what you really want and what you settled for or were oblivious to in the past.

You already have the seven crucial items for your list, those are mandatory qualities for your life and there are hints at more. It's not obsessive to have fifty or more traits listed. Don't be afraid to list everything you think you want or need.

My secret? I had well over one hundred qualities and attributes on my shopping list. I am an expert shopper and I know it has to be on the list to make it into the world. Before I met the love of my life, I met other guys who just weren't right for me. After a few really bad relationships, I decided to create a shopping list with all of the qualities, traits and characteristics that were solid, appealing and right for me. I listed everything. I listed everything I love, everything I think is important, and everything that I enjoy. Then I listed more. I added qualities I wanted in a man. I love to laugh and had to have a guy with a great sense of humor. I knew I wanted a guy who was spiritual. I love art and music, so he had to love those, too. I described how he would treat me, and how we would be together and put it on my list. I listed over one hundred traits and I checked the list after every date I had with a guy. If my date didn't have the qualities on my list, then he wasn't the guy for me. That's how I knew that when I met my husband, the love of my life, he was the one. I checked the list. My husband checked positive for all but two of them. The two qualities on the list that he didn't have, I put on the list because I thought they would please my mother. They really didn't matter. I knew I had the right guy. With your *Shopping For A Man* list, I know you can have yours too.

You can start your Shopping For A Man list, today. I prepared a special worksheet for you that will help you create your shopping list. (Download this resource at www.shoppingforaman.com.) I'm going to guide you and help you see new traits and ways of thinking and being that you can add to your list. What's great about your list is that not only do you discover what you really want in a guy, you also discover what's very important in your life.

*"I've been heartbroken. I've broken hearts.*
*That's part of life, and its part of figuring out*
*who you are so you can find the right partner."*
*Heidi Klum*

## Creating Your List

There are two ways that can easily help you write your *Shopping For A Man* list. One way to learn the qualities of the right guy for you is to look at what you don't like in guys you know or in relationships around you. Sounds backwards, but sometimes, you know more about what you don't like, then what you want.

One way to uncover some of the qualities you need, is to examine what was missing in your last relationships. They didn't work for one reason or another, so you know which things hurt you, troubled you or were plainly incompatible. Look at one of your past relationships. Maybe he hated all of your friends and constantly told you of all their bad qualities. Was he pessimistic or was he just trying to run your life and gain control? Look there and see what bothered you.

When you see a quality that you don't like or that didn't work for you, put the quality you do want on the list. At first, it will look like you're just writing down the bad stuff. This is a positive list of what you want. You're going to turn everything around. If he continually put you down, transform the negative quality into a positive that you want. Write that he compliments you and knows your worth. If he was lazy and you ended up doing all the work, whether it was to maintain the relationship or pay the bills, write that he is conscientious, a good worker and that he is always willing to help you. If all he wanted to do was what pleased him and didn't consider your needs, turn it around. You want someone who is considerate, thoughtful, attentive, loving, helpful, or any of the many adjectives and adverbs that will describe that man who cares about you. Get the worksheet you downloaded and list these qualities. You're going to update your list, so don't worry if your list is messy or doesn't make sense yet. Just keep on writing.

Our society does not give us very good role models for creating deep, bonded relationships. That's because it usually isn't dramatic and news; TV and film are all about the drama. Of course, you don't want a dramatic relationship. You want a fabulous, loving and fun relationship. If you look around, you'll get some great clues on what doesn't work, so you can select what does and put it on your list. While many times the topic in politics is all about family values, the political family is always calling each other names, bickering among themselves and trying to undermine each other for control. Well, if family is like that who wants to play there? No one is working for the fulfillment and benefit of the whole. If you know you are going jogging, that pair of high-heeled black pattern leather pumps should stay in the back of the closet. They don't work. They'll fall apart and get ruined. You must select the right shoe, the right model for a harmonious relationship.

### *Pick up your running shoes and feel free to break loose.*

Another way of building a quality list is to look at relationships that really work and have worked for a long time. Maybe you're still new at dating or you've only had a few dates or real relationships. Look at the relationships around you for examples and guidance. You may know one or two couples that get along fabulously. Look for a marriage or bonded situation of at least ten years. They've been through enough stuff to test their devotion and the everyday pragmatics of life. See how they act with each other. What do you notice about how he treats her? Do you see caring and love? Does he help her out in lots of different ways? Do they respect each other?

You can also ask them questions about what they think makes a good relationship and why those things are important. Look at it from their viewpoint. You're not looking for that particular man. You're looking at what qualities he brings into their lives. Ask her to describe her husband. Ask him questions about how they stayed together so long. What does he think are the most important things in their marriage? This will give you more qualities for your shopping list.

Building a relationship is building a realm to play in. You create a new country and then you both live there. What kind of country do you want to create? Do you want a loving, honorable and generally peaceful one? When life gets crazy do you want a haven from the madness? Your shopping list is vital. You are building your new world. You need all the materials. If you want a sound structure, you have to design the building. You need a solid roof, efficient plumbing, working doors and windows, so you better get good construction materials. You also need the manpower to build this world with you. You are looking for a partner, someone who is ready, willing and able to take on this lifetime project. You might find him in the hardware department. That's a great idea! Carpenters never go shopping without their list and neither should you.

The list you are writing is your shopping list. Can you see what is not working in your life and in other people's lives? Good. It's important to know what doesn't work. If you bought a toaster, and it didn't work, you'd take it back to the store. Maybe you'd exchange it for another toaster from the same company. If this one didn't work either, you'd take it back to the store and get a refund. The toaster is faulty. It doesn't perform the way you want.

It's the same thing with a relationship. You went shopping and bought a man with certain qualities. It didn't turn out well. So, you went right out again and you found another man. Well, you probably brought home the same thing in a different package. That didn't work either. Why? You hadn't learned how to shop yet. You didn't have a real working shopping list full of qualities and non-negotiables that would get you shopping in the right direction, for the right guy.

## MORE ON THE LIST?

What about adding tender, compassionate and joyful? Maybe you need dedicated, straightforward and strong.

Do you need pampering? How about a man who will cook dinner for you and then wash the dishes himself?

How about a man who will take care of you, and when you're feeling a little off, he cleans the house and runs you a bath?

Your list can take you a long time to assemble. It isn't fair to pressure yourself into thinking you know what you want. That's relatively unlikely since you haven't found him. Give yourself some time to explore what qualities you really want in a man, and a partner. You will continually add to your list as you see those qualities in others. Something that seemed unimportant may become a vital necessity. Other qualities that seemed crucial may be another illusion about yourself or the world that you haven't cleared up yet.

Money is a good example of dilemmas on your list. Often times what interests women more are the inner qualities of the man. They look for that deeply sensitive, emotional man who knows how they feel in their deepest hearts. Perfect. Then, just when they think that all is going so brilliantly, she finds out that this man hops from job to job faster than a rabbit. He is out of work more often than in.

Now, the dilemma. She wants a sensitive man, but she knows that bills must get paid. She is doing more of the cooking and hardly any dining out. Does she ignore this pattern? Does she cook and entertain for him, because he has no money? Is she getting tired of doing a lot of the work, but feeling guilty that she is focused on money and not his personal attributes? Does she dine out with her women friends because she is dying to have a meal out in the world somewhere? It's one thing to pay attention to finances. It's another to dress down and become the provider when that's not what you want.

This is not gold digging. This is not being excessively concerned with his financial worth. She works a full time job to keep her life in order. He is dancing at the whim of the universe. There is nothing wrong with either approach unless you are choosing a partner. You may be able to overlook this when you are dating and get all caught up in the passion and romance.

Later, when he can't take you to dinner and a movie, things may look very different. Much later, if you live together, his contribution to the living expenses may be significantly less than yours. You may be paying all the rent and most of the food bills for two people while his sensitive nature explores the deep undulations of his emotions. Is this what you want? It's not about where you shop. It's about whether you want to always shop in that particular store. Look at this aspect of your list for your comfort level and expectations. Don't judge yourself one way or the other. It isn't important whether you love blue or red. Red is not better than blue, but red may enhance your complexion or blue may bring out the color in your eyes. It is important to recognize your preferences, choices and comfort level and add them to your shopping list.

I'm going to remind you of the pitfalls in dating, so you can find and date a great guy. You're shopping. If he doesn't have the qualities you need and want, qualities that will complement you, support you and help you grow to be a better person, he's not the guy for you. That's great. If you know the store doesn't carry the brand of shoes you want, you just don't have to shop there.

### QUALITIES, TRENDS, AND LIFESTYLE

Here are more questions that can help you see qualities, trends, and lifestyle that feel right to you.

What do you like to do?

What are your best qualities?

What do you do for fun?

What is really interesting to you?

What are your goals and dreams for the future?

Do you want to have children?

Do you like to travel?

What do you need in a relationship?

What qualities and personality traits do you admire? (Think positive. Respectful, honest, generous, loyal, creative, kind etc.)

Keep adding your insights onto the list and read it over. This is a magical shopping list. Once you know what you want, you can start to shop for it. Make copies of it to use later. As you continue to shop, you'll find that you don't stop to pick up unnecessary items. You'll see your tastes change and your savvy grow. Of course, it's not enough to have the list. You have to use it. Every time you date a guy, you have to learn if he's right for you. Refer to the qualities on your list and see. You may be pleasantly surprised. He may have even better traits than you listed!

---

*Your shopping list is your best friend.*

# Visualization and Affirmation:
# ATTRACTING YOUR QUALITY GUY

Now, that you've started your *Shopping For A Man* list and you're becoming Consummate Consumer, you can do the next visualization and affirmation to begin to attract the guy who has those special qualities. This new visualization will start your real shopping intentions so you know what you want and are ready to go shopping. After all, without the list it's all just random.

Start with the "3 Steps To Centering" exercise. Then go on to the **Attracting Your Quality Guy Visualization**. This visualization helps you create the possibility and opportunity to attract your quality guy. Your Quality Guy is the one who has the qualities you need, want and admire.

# Visualization:
# Attracting Your Quality Guy

Take a deep breath.
Imagine yourself in a beautiful garden. There are beautiful flowers, large shade trees and you can hear the fountain splashing. You're in this garden to reflect on and attract a quality guy.

Think about your shopping list. Think about the qualities that you appreciate. You wrote these on your list.
As you go through them in your thoughts, smile.

Take another slow deep breath and say to yourself,
"I am ready to attract a Quality Guy."
"I am ready to be my true self and meet the guy who will love me, cherish me and complement my life."

Let the images, thoughts and feelings that this statement brings up just roll through you.

Take another breath and say to yourself,
"I am ready to attract a Quality Guy."
Keep smiling. You started the process in your list and in your life.

Congratulations. You learned about being a Consummate Consumer. You started to create your *Shopping For A Man* list to discover what's really important to you. You're looking at what qualities are important to you, in your own standards and integrity and the qualities you love and admire.  Now, you're ready to have some fun.

Now, smile.
You have a deeper understanding of yourself and you just made room for a fabulous guy to enter your life!

# Affirmation and Intention: Creating the Opening

Use this affirmation to increase and support your positive energy and outlook about dating. Try it right now and feel your new strength, freedom and open-minded perspective.

Take a slow deep breath.
Smile and say,

*"I create the opening right now for a great guy
to come into my life.
"I am open to meeting and dating a really great guy."*

Congratulations.
Now you're ready to learn about power shopping.

# POWER SHOPPING

Your list is relatively complete for now. You've cleaned out the closet to make some room for a new start. It's time to start using your shopping skills. When you go for groceries you have your list and refer to it, to make sure you get what you want. You are going to refer to this list every time you date a man. Make several copies to check off the supplies. Keep the list in your night table, lingerie drawer, or anywhere you will see it often and can chart your progress. I kept mine in my night table and checked it right after each date. Checking your list right after a date will keep you honest.

You're ready to get out there and learn to be a power shopper. A power shopper has a keen eye, knows quality when she sees it, knows what she is looking for and still can be a little flexible to make sure she doesn't overlook something surprising and wonderful.

---

*Dating is like shopping for shoes.*
*Always look for quality, fit and style.*
*The right guy and the right shoes make life fabulous.*

Now it's fun time. Let's do more shopping! Find some place to shop and meet guys where you are comfortable. This is an excursion into the world's trading centers. You are out there to have fun and to hone your skills. You've begun busting up those illusions. You are ready to sit back, listen to who is out there, and read the labels.

When you decide that you are shopping for a man, it just isn't as loaded as when you're seeking that lifetime mate. The whole conversation and reality shifts. You can relax. He's out there. You don't have to push and shove. Just sit on a comfortable perch and see who comes along. It can be anywhere. Good choices? What do you enjoy? Art galleries? Sports? Dancing? Theater? Lectures? Online dating? There are thousands of things to do out there as well as the classic bars and clubs.

# MODES FOR SHOPPING

## Scanning Mode

You are going to check out everyone. Your approach is that you are a vibrant, interesting, gorgeous woman who is available to meet a charming, appropriate man. You know what you're looking for and what qualities you have in mind. You have no idea what package the merchandise will arrive in, but with your list, you'll know it when you see it.

This is scanning mode. You are simply scanning a room, looking over the people from a distance. When you go into a great shop you stand somewhere, near the front door, in the center of the room or off to one side close to the front and you scan the room for the items that intrigue you. You're not connecting with anything first. This is getting the lay of the land. Where are the dresses? Where are the gorgeous shoes? Where are the hidden treasures? That is scanning mode.

Scanning Mode gives you a sense of the whole room. You can see the faces of people who might interest you. You can notice if there is one charming man standing near the door or several great guys all looking at a particular sculpture at the gallery opening. This is all about a view at a distance to see what is happening and where the people are that you may find interesting. In Scanning Mode you want to watch the guys and how they interact and how they relate to the people around them. If you're at a social place, a bar, disco or club are the guys smiling? Are they having fun? If you're at an event that is more subdued, a gallery, conference, community event then scan and see if the guys are friendly. Are they listening to their group talk? Is he leading the conversation or listening? Is he laughing or intense? Everything in Scanning Mode gives you an overview so you can navigate in this environment.

## Browsing Mode

Browsing Mode gives you a little closer view. When you're browsing the store, you're getting closer to the items. You may go right up to the counter with all the best cosmetics. You're not picking them up and trying them out. You're just looking closer without any attachment, just intrigue. You're walking over to the jewelry counter and casually looking in the cases. You check out the gorgeous gold bracelets that have the carved jade designs. You make a mental note to remember them and see if it intrigues you. Then you go over to see the newest handbags. Browsing Mode is an easy and casual stroll for a closer view before any real conversation or connections are made.

Since you don't know what Quality Guy looks like or where you'll meet, you're browsing to see if you have any interest. You're also looking to see where you may like to land first. Do you want to go over to the bar, stand near the band or just stroll?

Browsing Mode lets you stroll closer to him. So if there are several guys that look interesting or you see a group of people that seem fun and nice, then you can get closer and listen a bit. You can smile and nod or say hello. If you've already chosen your spot, the place you're going to sit, stand or perch, then browsing mode gives you a great view and the opportunity to be welcoming to those guys or that guy who is already intriguing.

It's a shopper's dream! That irresistible treasure can be anywhere and you know you are going to find it. That's why you're shopping for a man.

Now, you need some shoppers' clues, some insider tips that will help you recognize a good deal when you see one and avoid damaged goods right away. This is your Power Shopping training.

*"When it comes to men, deal with them as they
are, not how you'd like them to be."*
*Greg Behrendt*

# MEETING AND DATING

## Good Clues, Bad Clues and Smart Shoppers

Your first encounter with a guy, even your first hello, gives you lots of information. These 5 Powerful Clues are guidelines to help you be a better shopper. What happens in that meeting gives you a first impression. It also gives you clues, sometimes good clues and sometimes bad clues, about the guy. Your first impressions, the clues you receive, whether they are revealed in what he says or how he acts with you, are vital info that helps you decide whether this outfit is going to work. Think about shopping for a new dress. Across the room, it may look exciting. When you get closer, maybe not so much.

Good Clues let you know there are positive indications. Bad Clues let you know that this will not work out for you. Smart Shoppers use these clues to make decisions right away. When you have Good Clues, you know that you have evidence that this guy has good qualities that you like. When you get Bad Clues, this guy is not showing you the qualities you need and want in a date or in a man. Smart Shoppers learn the clues and save themselves valuable shopping time, so they can move on to a better fit. No sense in hanging around the dress racks thinking about how you can make a shirtwaist dress work for you when there's a great little mini dress displayed on another rack.

## CLUE ONE: Approach
You are sitting at a bar and someone offers to buy you a drink. Great. He's noticed you and will introduce himself. How does he approach you and what does he look at?

## GOOD CLUE

He looks at your face, smiles and introduces himself. He asks your name. He asks you if he can sit down. He asks if he can buy you a drink and then asks what you are having. He gets the bartender's attention, orders and still makes easy conversation with you.

Once you have your drink he asks a few questions, shares about himself and watches for clues from you to continue. This is a good clue. He seems attentive, real, and polite. That's all you need to know right now, so that's good.

## BAD CLUE

If he looks at your breasts first, throw him back right away. He has to look at your face. Some people have difficulty making strong eye contact, but if he doesn't make any eye contact or look at your face while talking to you, it's a sure sign he has something else on his mind. It may or may not be sex. Whatever it is, he's distracted. If he isn't paying attention to you now, even before he knows you, what will happen later? Just smile and watch.

This one is probably not a keeper. He is either more interested in looking at your physical attributes or very self-absorbed. First meetings and first dates are important. If someone is not very convincing on their first encounter, toss them back on the rack. It's just not a fit for you and you don't even have to think about it.

## SMART SHOPPERS

A first encounter and a first date is the time to impress you. Guys are on their best behavior. No one wants rejection before they even begin. So if he doesn't want interesting conversation, if he bought you a drink figuring you'll leave with him because he's a man and he's clean, give him a big ironic smile. Be polite and let him go gracefully into that good night, alone.

Unfortunately, some men buy women a drink just so they don't look as if they're alone in the bar. You are sitting next to a man at the bar. He thinks since he bought you a drink, that you're going to stick around, at least until you've finished. There are no rules that say you have to stay if he's not charming. You can leave anytime. You can take your drink and go off, never to return. You're shopping. Who says you have to stay in the same department when you don't see what you want?

If he's rude at anytime, leave. Don't apologize. Don't excuse yourself. Get off the chair and go somewhere else. It can be as simple as a comment that makes you uncomfortable or a derogatory statement. Doesn't matter. If you don't like what's being sold, you don't buy it. It's that simple.

Safety note: Anytime you are in a situation that gets out of hand, ask for help. If someone is rude and you want to leave, ask someone who works at the place to walk you out. In this instance it could be the manager, the bar tender, the bouncer or a waitperson. Just have someone accompany you to your car or a cab, and leave. It's important to be safe.

## CLUE TWO: Connection

He's bought you the drink or you've given him the okay to chat and you are in conversation. Right away you can see if you have a connection with him. How is the initial conversation? Do you have eye contact?

### *GOOD CLUE*

Right away you can feel that he is attentive. He's still looking at you and asking easy questions. He seems interested in what you have to say and, what's more interesting right now, is his attention. He's easy, calm and warm. He's not trying to prove anything.

It's only been about five minutes and you have smiled or laughed several times. You like his smile, he laughs easily and nothing seems really forced or too intense. This is the initial connection. It's not about bells and whistles. It's about easy connection. You already know he's interested by his warm voice, the questions he asks you, how he looks in your eyes and how relaxed he is. You're shopping for a man, so of course, you want to be comfortable and having fun.

### *BAD CLUE*

You are talking to him and so far in the first thirty minutes he hasn't asked you any questions about yourself or your thoughts.

Right now, his interest is himself, rather than in you. If the conversation fascinates you, then just keep listening. Listening is an art. We can learn some incredible things if we just sit back and listen to someone else. Besides, you have time. You're out shopping and this is part of the fun. Don't think about whether he's right for you yet. At least he has some interesting things to say.

If he's complaining about something, he's dumping. This is self-absorbed behavior and not a very good start to any encounter. If he's not interesting, if he's annoying, complaining or just irritating, there's no need to hang around. Obviously, there isn't anything interesting for you to browse through in this department.

## SMART SHOPPERS

If you are having a great time, then keep the conversation going. It's very early to make decisions, so keep it light and easy. Right now, you're still giving him permission to keep talking and to get to know you a little better. No heavy conversations. No penetrating questions. Have fun, be genuine, chat and listen.

If he's rude, or if you're uncomfortable, it's okay to leave. You don't have to listen politely. Just smile and leave. If he's like this when you first meet, then you'll hear much more complaining, annoying and boring conversation later. It doesn't matter if he's lonely and just wants to talk. You are window-shopping right now. How long can you stand in front of a window that has nothing in it?

# CLUE THREE: Conversation

It's been over an hour. He's still there. You're both still talking away. You are learning more about him and sharing more about yourself.

## GOOD CLUE

He's sharing a little about himself and asking you questions. You are enjoying yourself and enjoying him.

This is a light conversation after all you just met. It's not heavy, not political and not demanding. He's still looking at you, your eyes, your face, and he is smiling and engaging. It's a good and interesting conversation. You do find him interesting. You are getting to know more about him and you're beginning to like him.

He seems to be a pretty happy guy, already shared a little bit about his job and his interests and you don't see anything inappropriate that will ruin your shopping experience. Good news, so far.

## BAD CLUE

He is asking more questions than he is answering. Every time you ask something, he gives a quick or an evasive answer. Then he asks you more questions and you keep talking away.

As skeptical as it may sound, what is he hiding? It's true that you are a fascinating person. No question. Most people want to talk about themselves, but in this case It doesn't appear that he wants to share anything about himself with you. Is he just gathering information about you? Is he hiding the fact that he's married or committed and just wants to pass the time? It's okay if that's true. You are shopping. You have to know whether the items that interest you are available for purchase.

If the conversation is pleasant and you're having fun, that is great. Just remember your intention is to find a suitable partner. If you keep this in mind then you can have a wonderful conversation with everyone. You won't feel the desperate need to take home something from the mall, at the end of the day.

### SMART SHOPPERS

You are really enjoying his company. The conversation is going great. What does great mean? He's sharing about himself. You're sharing about yourself. He complements you and it's genuine. This is starting to give you an idea whether you would be interested in continuing a conversation with him later. Is he smart? Is he charming? Is he funny? Do you already have some shared interests? This is starting to look interesting and fun. If you like, you can stick around for more.

If he is deflecting your questions and avoiding answering your questions then, really, don't bother with him. If you get no clear response, let it go. He is hiding something. If he tells you that you are fascinating, just smile and thank him. Then tell him that you want to know about him. You can even let him know that you think he's evading the questions if you feel comfortable with that. The only people who can get away with this kind of conversation are Oprah, Dr. Phil, Steve Harvey, Diane Sawyer, Tavis Smiley, Jon Stewart and Katie Couric and that's because it's an interview, not a conversation.

Unless you're getting paid for this interview, keep shopping. If you have to try too hard now, forget it. He may or may not open up later. This is like shopping for clothes that don't have any labels. Is it silk or cotton or poly? Is this an outfit you want to take home?

How do you know? It's a little boring to be the one who carries the conversation, unless you really know that you want the silent type.

## CLUE FOUR: Comfort Level

You are getting to know him better. It's been over an hour and maybe even several hours. Are you still comfortable with this man? Does he make you feel at ease, relaxed, interested and appreciated?

### GOOD CLUE

He really is interested in you in a relaxed way. He's sharing more about himself, and you're getting to know him better. He's not sharing details that are too personal or opinionated. He's asking you questions and the conversation is going really well. You can see he has a good sense of humor. He's bright and intelligent. He's caring. He's opening up and you're getting to see that he has few of the qualities you listed on your shopping list. You're already seeing some positive evidence of who he is and you like it.

You are interested in the topics of the conversation. You both have one or two shared interests, so you can contribute to the conversation and bring a little more depth there.

The initial conversation for meeting someone is cordial, polite chat. In this chat he's asking you permission to enter your realm, your space and meet you. Then, as time goes by, you start to talk about more interesting or slightly more personal topics. Freedom is the key. You and he are free to leave the conversation at any time, for any reason.

### BAD CLUE

He is coming on very strong. He is sitting more than close and monopolizing the conversation with you. He's very opinionated and strong.

Ask yourself why this man is so intense. A first meeting can become very dynamic, but only after a long time. What are the underlying motivations for his actions? Looking at someone's underlying motivations is not being paranoid. It's important to have a mode of healthy observation. What makes him want to hold your exclusive attention and create a barrier, saying others are not welcome?

If he asks you too many personal questions in your first meeting, that may not be appropriate. He may ask about what you do, but why does he want to know where you work or how you feel about your mother? Why did he ask about any previous marriages? These are too personal for an initial meeting.

You don't have to answer these questions. Your thoughts and your life are private experiences that you choose to share with others. You don't have to satisfy the curiosity of someone you barely know, just because they ask you and it could be dangerous to tell a stranger where you live or work.

## SMART SHOPPERS

Smart Shoppers are attentive. You are shopping. This is just the stage of looking at the displays and seeing if anything intrigues you this season.

If you are having a great time, then it signals the opportunity for more. The conversation is light and interesting, and that can show you his personality. You're getting a look at how he is and what interests him. Good. He's sharing time with you. He's attentive to the conversation and asks questions about what interests you. Now you are receiving positive signals, not only that he likes you, but that he has qualities that you admire and desire in a guy. You have almost enough info to say yes, if he asks to see you again and wants your number.

He seems too intense. He's jumping off the rack and trying to get into your bag. If he encroaches on too much intimacy, just back off. Smile, but keep your distance. Check this man out and ask yourself why he is being this intense. No one likes a hard sell or a pushy sales person. He could have any number of motives. Proceed gently. You don't really have to figure out why he is so intense so quickly. Asking yourself why makes you more attentive. Don't get absorbed into the drama and intensity. Sit back. Watch. You just have to ask yourself one question, "Does this work for me?"

Remember, you are going to see who this man is by watching his interactions. He is showing you clues and evidence about himself. Smart shoppers pay attention to all the little and big clues sent out.

# CLUE FIVE: Intuition

Intuition is your inner knowing. You are receiving messages, feelings and deeper clues that are seriously telling you something. Pay attention to those gut feelings, impressions and your woman's intuition. I'm an expert in this and I know above all, that this is very important. Please do not disregard this special gift. If you feel weird for no reason, then understand that something deeper, an intuitive message is coming to you. Don't disregard these messages and feelings. Think of them as a special gift that can lead you in the right direction in dating and in life.

### GOOD CLUE

There is something about this guy that you really like. You can't put your finger on it, but he makes you happy. You've been listening, watching and you like the conversation and the guy. This feels positive and easy. Your intuition is telling you something positive.

### BAD CLUE

You are not feeling comfortable. In fact you are feeling nervous and not in a good way. It feels wrong and you don't know why. You don't know why, but you're trying to find a way to leave. This does not feel right and you are uncomfortable with this man. Your intuition is telling you something negative.

### SMART SHOPPERS

Pay attention to your intuition. It's vital. Some people call this a gut feeling, because often time you sense it in your stomach or your solar plexus. It's another way of knowing if you're getting inner guidance. The more you pay attention to your intuition the better your intuition works.

Do you have a good feeling about this guy? Is this feeling light and happy and making you smile? If you feel really guided to see this guy again, then follow your intuition and say yes if he asks you.

If you have a bad feeling, if you're feeling weird or creepy vibes or feel nervous, tense or fearful, the answer is NO! Do not worry if it's not polite. Do not second-guess yourself. This is your intuition telling you something. There are lots of ways to politely tell someone you're not interested, so do that. If that doesn't work, then take steps for your personal comfort and safety.

# FIRST DATE WARDROBE ESSENTIALS

## Your Shopping List in Action

The first encounter has gone well. Congratulations. He is single and available. You are interested. He is interested. You have arranged a second meeting. A date? Great. All the rules of your first meeting apply. Both of you have upped the ante. You have decided to get to know each other a little better. He's asked you out or you've mutually set another meeting.

First date. This is an exploratory meeting. Learn a bit more about each other and have fun. No expectations. Don't indulge in fantasies about a condo together in Manhattan or a little farm in Nebraska. The rules of shopping still apply. Cordial conversation and interesting chats are the mode. You are both together to enjoy each other and see if you feel comfortable and compatible. So far, so good. You wouldn't have accepted the invitation unless you already had some good clues about this guy.

Every first date has its own form. Every meeting place has its own social environment. It's different at a party, a conference, a health club, a gallery, a bar, or a lecture. One thing that is necessary for every first date is cordial conversation. Cordial conversation helps you get to know the guy and see how well you connect and get along. I know this sounds easy and basic, but so many women ignore this just because they want to impress, or he's so cute or they are a little lonely.

*Looking for love in all the wrong places?*
*Why would you shop for shoes in a hardware store?*

Be clear about the kind of guy you want. You have your shopping list. It's all shopping and you are in charge. You know some of the qualities you want. Now you're getting a little more aware of the merchandise and whether it fits your lifestyle. It's that easy. Dresses come and go. Shoes look good on the display and then they don't when you get closer. That's the intrigue and delight of shopping. Sometimes, the jacket that doesn't look like much from across the aisle turns out to be the best deal you ever found.

What you are looking for, in very general terms, is someone who is cordial and social, who enjoys your company. You want a pleasant and interesting conversation. You want to know a little more about him, enough to find out the general likes and tastes in his life. You want him to ask you questions and listen to your answers. You want to see and hear that this man wants to know what you have to say, and that he wants to learn more about you. You want him to share general things about himself, so you can know him a little better. This is all very lightweight, but highly important. The first date is not the time for the soul's intimate revelations. More information can come later, if you decide that you want more.

These are the clues you are investigating in each meeting. You are checking out the color of the dress. You are wondering about the manufacturer. So, out of all the dresses in the "Great Galactic Shopping Mall Of Love," you noticed a particular dress that seems intriguing. That is as far as you've come. You haven't even taken it off the rack yet. You are still in Shopper's Scanning Mode.

When you agree to have some conversation, you get a little closer to the dress. Now, you can look at the cut. You find out whether it has buttons or a zipper, long or short sleeves. You will notice the general blend of the fabric. It may look like linen. Maybe it's a cotton/linen blend. Of course, it could be rayon or even raw silk. It's too soon to tell. You really have to touch it to get more information and the first date isn't the touching stage. I'm not talking about physical intimacy. I'm talking about how much you will really know about this guy or that dress at this stage. This is the stage of restrained, polite interest. You have no commitment to take the dress off the rack, and you are definitely not taking it into the dressing room.

Cordial conversation, wherever that takes place, will give you vast amounts of information about this person. Social distance is important. It's a dance of permission.

The first date is about deeper conversation and looking at the possibility of connection. When you feel good about the conversation, you let this person know that he can stay a little longer and talk some more. This doesn't mean that you are dating him. It means that you are willing to give him more time to get to know you, and you him. No matter how the evening turns out, at every moment, you are free to walk away. Just because you walked into the store, doesn't mean you need to stay or browse. You can leave at any time.

Each person has their own boundaries. They stem from family and cultural upbringing and become more personal as she matures. For some, hugging is a very intimate expression of closeness and not appropriate for everyone she meets. Some people hug everyone. Some people stand very close to each other. This can be alarming to someone else who keeps several feet in distance. Know your boundaries. They will loosen when you are comfortable. If he is standing far away from you, give him time to feel more comfort. If he is standing too close, back up. Let him know that you are not comfortable with that yet.

The first date will show you if he meets you with interest, warmth and respect. Anything less is unacceptable. You will find all of this out in his tone of voice and his topic of conversation. You will see it in how attentive or distracted he is towards you. The clues show up everywhere. A Power Shopper uses all of her skills. She is attentive to any hype about the goods that may be unfounded. She watches with interest. She looks at things carefully. She listens to the sales pitch and makes decisions based on what she wants. The merchandise reveals everything to you, and you decide which items warrant a further look.

# FIRST DATE REVELATIONS

## Nine Signs of Fabulous or Flawed

All the general rules of interpersonal relations apply. He must be considerate. He must treat you with respect. If at any time the respect falters, grab your shopping bag and go. If he doesn't respect you now, how can you expect it later?

This is your first date. He should be on his absolute best behavior. He's supposed to wow you. You're supposed to dazzle him. That's the courting game. If he isn't pleasant on this date, forget it. If that brand new sweater in the store doesn't flatter you right away, it's not going to look better with age. People don't get more polite once they know you better. People don't give out respect because you have done something to deserve it. Respect is a way to approach all people. It is honoring the life of another. If you don't have sure clues of respect in these first dates, you probably never will.

Respect is a matter of degrees. There are no concrete rules. The dictionary definition of respect is: to regard and appreciate. Honor and esteem. For a working definition, respect is being considerate, polite, interested and acting appropriate to the situation. It's up to you to figure out the respect ratio. The 9 Signs of Fabulous or Flawed below show you some major things to notice when you're on your first date. Sign of Fabulous shows some actions that will make you happy and show you there is a possibility of a great guy. Sign of Flawed shows actions considered suspect. These are warnings to beware. Use the 9 Signs of Fabulous or Flawed, as your shopping guidelines and you'll have more success.

### SIGN OF FABULOUS ONE
**He's right on time for the date. He is smiling and happy to impress.**
This means he is considerate. He appreciates you and will not make you wait or waste your time. It also shows you he is happy and ready to go on a date with you. That means he's showing his focus, reliability and interest in you. This is fabulous.

### SIGN OF FLAWED ONE
**He's more than five minutes late, he didn't call and he's not bleeding or limping.**

This means he wasn't seriously injured. So, he has no valid excuse for being late. He already knew you were going out. There may be some hidden reasons for being late.

He didn't think about the date. He didn't plan his time. He forgot until the last minute. He got caught up at work. He's terminally late.

Any of these signs of flawed and hundreds more, hint at where he considers you in the importance ratio. This is your first date. If you are not a primary concern now, then when both of you are further along and more comfortable in the relationship you'll be very low on the scale of priorities. This is flawed.

## SIGN OF FABULOUS TWO
**He dressed well.**
Love it when a man looks great. This means he takes pride in himself and he wants to make a good impression. That's good. You want him to make a good impression on you. This also suggests he was thinking of you. He was thinking of your date and looking forward to your time together. It also suggests that he spent some time getting ready for this date. All good news. This is fabulous.

## SIGN OF FLAWED TWO
**He dressed like a slob.**
He told you where you are going and he didn't dress appropriately for the situation. This could be anything from not being showered to ripped, dirty jeans for an elegant dinner. You are the judge here.

Your level of comfort doesn't seem to matter to him. This is not a judgment of the financial status of the clothing. It's not about designer fashion. How he dresses reflects how important he feels you are at this time. This is a big clue about whether he wants to impress you with his manners and show you he is considerate. If he doesn't want to impress you now, what will happen later? If he's not willing to show himself off in his best light now, wait until things heat up a bit. This is flawed.

## SIGN OF FABULOUS THREE
**He is listening to what you are saying in the conversations.**
He is smiling as you talk. He is listening in the conversation. You can see by what he says, how he responds and how he's looking at you that he is interested in you and in what you are saying. You may

have to get some conversation rhythms going or not. If he's listening and attentive, that's important. Remember your shopping list? You want a man who listens to you. This is fabulous.

## SIGN OF FLAWED THREE
**He doesn't listen to what you are saying.**
You're talking about something and he's looking around the room, or gazing off into space, or just nodding his head. You know he's not paying attention to you.

It doesn't matter why. He's just not good company. You want someone who listens to you, whether they agree or not. This is your life and your time. Not listening is not good. Now you know he doesn't listen and so there's no need to waste any time with this guy. If he isn't interested right this minute, he won't be after a few months. This is flawed.

## SIGN OF FABULOUS FOUR
**He genuinely compliments you in conversation.**
He is listening to what you say and compliments your insight and understanding. He notices your personal interests and makes genuine comments and truly flattering remarks about what you are saying. It's not all flattery. This is real. You can feel that he gets something about you that impresses him. Your definitely want a guy who recognizes how great you are right away. This is a plus. This is fabulous.

## SIGN OF FLAWED FOUR
**He belittles you in conversation.**
This can be anything. He makes an off-handed comment about how you look. It's not flattering. He shakes his head when you tell him what you think, as if you have no clue about it. He puts you down in some way. These comments can be really overt by telling you that you don't know what you are talking about or by saying something mildly cruel that hurts your feelings. It can be a look, a throw away comment, a demeaning phrase.

Move on, darling. These are going to be the most painful shoes you ever tried on. They pinch your toes, and rub at the back of your heel and you wobble in them. All you'll get are corns, calluses and blisters. Leave these in the store and run. This is flawed.

## SIGN OF FABULOUS FIVE
**He engages in the conversation.**
He asks you questions. He answers questions and volunteers information about himself.

He is easy going in conversation. He's sharing about himself in an open, but casual way. He is very interested in you, too. He asks questions without prying. You feel really comfortable with his ideas. How he acts shows you that he is open and responsive. He engages in conversation. It's not forced, controlling or directing you. This is good. While you can help guide someone in conversation and this may not be a deciding factor in shopping for a man, it goes a long way. This is a pattern for the long term. This is fabulous.

## SIGN OF FLAWED FIVE
**He talks about himself all night long.**
You've heard about his job, how great he is, how much money he makes, his 'ex' and all the rest. He is bragging up a storm.

Yes, he's trying to impress you. He wants you to think he is the best deal in the store. Too much hype is suspect. He may be insecure or have an over inflated ego. Who cares! He's not really interested in you. He wants to know what you think about him. He is self-centered. He will require too much maintenance.

You may have to constantly minister to his needs and wants, while you take care of your own, because he'll never see them. He's too busy being consumed with himself.

In the flip side of this situation he talks about himself, but instead of bragging, he complains about everything. His wife left him. No one understands him. Pain, suffering, the overly sensitive, tortured man tries to get your sympathy, but this is boring conversation. The same care instructions apply. It's just a different garment. Pass. Put this right back on the rack and keep browsing. This garment requires too much attention and care. This is flawed.

## SIGN OF FABULOUS SIX
**He considers what you say and gives opinions when appropriate.**
He listens to what you say and when he agrees with you, he lets you know. Of course, he doesn't always agree with you and that is important. He's secure enough with himself to speak about and

share differing opinions. Your opinion on politics is not the same as his, but you can tell he can consider your point of view and respect it. That's okay, because you don't agree with everything he says either. But there are things you both could learn from the differing points of view. This is open. This is fabulous.

## SIGN OF FLAWED SIX
**He agrees or disagrees with everything you say.**
Your ideas about politics are amazing. Your opinion on politics is ridiculous. How ingenious, you eat burgers and fries for lunch. How did you think of that? Your taste in food is not very sophisticated. Whatever you bring up in conversation is either an argument or pandering. This behavior is not going to happen with the same guy, but it's the same annoying pattern. This may be tiresome for a relationship. This man is that pair of jeans that is two sizes too small. You have to really pull on them, just to get into them. You have to lie down on the bed to pull them on and zip them. Then you worry about how much you can eat before they burst. He is too much trouble and not worth the effort. This is flawed.

## SIGN OF FABULOUS SEVEN
**He takes you somewhere really great.**
He mentioned that he wanted to take you somewhere special and he did. He put a lot of thought into this date. He wants you to have a great time. How did he decide where to take you? After talking with you a few times, he thought you might like this place. After thinking about the places he really likes, he thought you would like this, too.

It doesn't matter if where you go is fancy or not, he chose a place because he thought you would like it, have a good time and appreciate it. Good. He gave this date serious thought. He wants to please you. Not only does this show he likes you, but you can see he is thoughtful, attentive and is happy to please you. Oh, yes. This is fabulous.

## SIGN OF FLAWED SEVEN
**He takes you somewhere really sleazy.**
Sleazy is in the eyes of the beholder. First, tell him you're uncomfortable and ask to leave. Suggest going to a place where you're comfortable.

So what is he saying about you and about himself? Well, he could be testing your comfort level to see if you can deal with a variety of situations. Too bad. This is rude behavior. You don't need testing. You're an adult and life has enough tests. This shows cockiness and lack of respect. It also shows a certain amount of contempt.

What if he actually hangs out in this place? Everyone knows his name and greets him warmly. You could stay for a little while to understand what he sees in it. But if this is what he's doing to impress you, this isn't a fit. You probably won't get roses for your birthday or a marriage proposal. Then again, if you like the idea of a boa constrictor and rats for Valentine's Day, this guy may be your dream dude. This is flawed.

## SIGN OF FABULOUS EIGHT
**He gives you his undivided attention and is really present.**
He likes talking to you with no distractions. His phone rang once and he apologized for not putting it on mute. You can see this date is important to him. He's not interested in having any distractions tonight. He says it. He values his time with you.

You want your first date to be special. You want to get to know him and share some quality time. The fact that he isn't distracted with all the toys shows you that he thinks you're important. You are being treated with respect and attention. Right away you know that when you need to talk, when you need his input or attention, he'll gladly give it. Perfect. This is fabulous.

## SIGN OF FLAWED EIGHT
**He makes calls, texts and posts to Facebook while he's with you the restaurant, movies, etc.**
You are in the middle of dinner and he pulls out his phone. He just has to make one quick call. He has to make an important call. It won't take long. He is texting someone. So he's looking down, distracted, and not paying attention to you.

Unless this man is a surgeon on call or a psychiatrist counseling suicidal patients, this is unacceptable behavior. It's unacceptable behavior for anyone - date, lover or friend, to talk on the phone while out with you. This is not their home. This is not their office. He is spending time with you. Yes, I know that lots of people do this and think it's all good. It still reveals where you are on the importance scale to him. If he has to do something else when he has committed his time to you, what does that say about him?

The first date is the time men are the most polite, the most generous with their attention and time. If you aren't getting undivided attention now, you may have to stand naked in his office to get some later. This is a good indication of what is to come. Reconsider.

If he's so fascinating that you want another date, ask him to put his phone away. You can say it quite pleasantly, but let him know this is not comfortable for you. If he gets annoyed with that, then you really know he's not worth a second glance. You don't even have to take this shirt off the rack. The sign is very clearly marked, Slightly Irregular Clearance. If he can handle your remarks and is willing to put away his stuff, you may want to give him another chance. Maybe he hasn't figured out the rules of consideration for dating and relating. This is flawed.

## SIGN OF FABULOUS NINE
**He planned a lovely evening and an added surprise.**
You're both enjoying the night. You are having fun and you can tell he is too. He asks you if you'd like to extend the evening and go to a great club to hear some music. They have a fantastic band and since he already knows your taste in music, would you like to go? Yes, of course you would. It's a pleasant surprise. It's a nice surprise that he remembered your music and that he made extra arrangements just in case.

He wasn't counting on you going, just hoping you might. He was anticipating that you would both enjoy each other's company. Actually he planned for it. He's showing you that he does plan for this to be something more, whatever that is. He wants to spend more time with you and this shows you that he is decisive, attentive, caring and likes to plan to make you happy. Are you smiling? This is fabulous.

## SIGN OF FLAWED NINE
**He has other plans for later in the evening that don't include you.**
He's given himself two hours for dinner and conversation then he has to meet someone later. He hopes you don't mind. This is a dinner date. Mind? Watch out.

This is a man who hedges his bets. Just in case you don't work out to be as enchanting as he hoped, this guy has something lined up for back up. He doesn't want to waste the evening.

He may tell you that he made these plans a long time ago and couldn't break them. Why didn't he pick another time or reschedule? He may say that he has business to do. Well, if he can't spare an evening to share with you this early on in a possible relationship, you will be alone for more time than you can count. It doesn't matter what the excuse. This is rude. It's a slap on the face, even if you don't know that your cheeks are tingling.

Use a shovel full of skepticism and be on alert. This man does not generate confidence. He doesn't trust you to be any more than a passing interest. He doesn't trust himself to be smart enough to pick a good woman. He is looking for the back door before any hope of a relationship begins. You can bet he'll use that exit whenever it's convenient. No possibility here. Someone wore this item and then returned it to the store. It's passing itself off as new goods. No sale! This is flawed.

The above are the Nine Signs of Fabulous and Flawed. They are behavioral patterns that show you exactly what you are scanning in the "Great Galactic Shopping Mall Of Love." This is only the first date! You are browsing. You still haven't taken anything off the rack. Signs of fabulous are potential. They let you recognize a man's good qualities. You may even see qualities that you forgot to put on your shopping list.

Flawed behavior is a big signal to drop the merchandise and leave the store. You are not looking for a guy to makeover. You are not shopping for a project and you don't want shoes that give you blisters. Just remember your shopping list. You're going to check that, right after your date.

# FIRST DATE'S AFTER-GLOW

With your first date completed, you can think about everything that happened. Now is the time to take out your list and make some notes. Don't leave your impressions to memory. Power Shopping is knowing what you want and having criteria for your purchases.

You are Power Shopping through your whole relationship, until you both make a solid commitment. When you both make a solid commitment, that's the deal.

Right now, you are nowhere near knowing. Do not take anything off the rack. Do not try it on. Do not fantasize about being married to him or having his children. There is no sense in dreaming about wearing that special dress that you see way across the room, until you know that it's your size, color and fit. You aren't there yet. Relax and enjoy. Just maintain the scanning mode and see what develops.

Pay attention to what is right in front of you. Three dates are the most you will need to discover whether dating this man has more serious potential. On the first date this man is on his best behavior. Any problems, any discourtesy is inexcusable. Whatever issues come up on the first date will multiply one hundred times in the course of a deeper relationship. Pay attention to that quiet voice that warns you. Listen to those alarm bells going off in your head. No sale! NO SALE!!

# IT'S ALL ABOUT THE STYLE AND FIT

He doesn't call after the first date. Sometimes things don't work for a reason. Maybe the chemistry isn't there. Don't get upset. So what! He saved you shopping time. Now, you don't even have to decide whether he's worthy of a second glance. He's not.

Some women do have a problem with this. It's a matter of self-esteem. Even if they didn't enjoy the date or the man, they can't believe that he didn't call and want more of them. A client of mine, Diana, could not believe that after a great first date, the guy never called back. No call and no text. Just empty space. She was almost obsessed with the rejection. She ruminated about everything that happened on the date, trying to see what went wrong. Did she say something weird or offensive? Was she too outspoken? Did she ask too many questions? Why didn't he call? Wasn't she good enough? She thought they really made a connection. He said he'd call.

During my conversation with Diana I said, "This is fantastic." She thought I was being sarcastic, so I clarified it. "You don't have to please him. You don't have to worry about him. This is great news. This is about him, not you. Now you know he's not the style and fit for you. You can find another great guy."

It took her a while to get it. It took her some time to realize that she could let it go, because it just didn't fit. She let go of the feelings of rejection and maybe a little anger, too. A month later, she started dating someone who was thrilled to be with her.

It's the same situation when a gal decides to sleep with a guy and then he doesn't call. She may not want to see this man again. She didn't have a good time. When he doesn't call, she gets frantic. This pushes all of her buttons. He should want her. She was great. She is great.

These are just buttons. She has some esteem problems. Rejection can hurt. She didn't want him as a relationship. She knew that from the beginning. When she discovers that he doesn't want her, then she goes into action. She rants and raves. Maybe she even chases him. She just cannot handle the fact that he's not interested.

*Wake Up. You are caught in a shopper's nightmare. Take a long deep breath of expensive boutique air and regroup.*

*It's all about the shopping.*

If this is you, if you've felt this way before, to quote Taylor Swift, "Shake it off." You stepped into a dating trap. You don't really want that hat on the mannequin. It isn't right for you. It's not even your style. But the sales person told you that you can't have it and now you have to have that hat. Now, you are frantic. You bargain with the clerk. It looked so good on you. What do you mean it's on hold for someone else? No way. You call the clerk, you call the store, you tell your friends and obsess about the hat that you really didn't want, but because you can't have it the allure is irresistible. This is only a dream. Step out of the nightmare in into the next boutique.

# VISUALIZATION AND AFFIRMATION: THE POWER SHOPPER

Now, that you've learned more about The 5 Powerful Clues for Your First Encounter of Meeting and Dating and learned about Good Clues, Bad Clues and Smart Shoppers you are gaining some real shopping expertise. When you add The 9 Signs of Fabulous or Flawed to your shopping skills, you have the major signs that will help you know if he has the qualities that are right for you. You want to make a heart connection with an appropriate guy. These new skills give you a great view and the wisdom to play.

You're becoming a Power Shopper. You can do the next visualization and affirmation to begin to attract the guy who has those special qualities. This new visualization will start your real shopping intentions so you know what you want and are ready to go shopping. After all, without the list it's all just random.

Start with "3 Steps To Centering" exercise so you can be immersed in the whole visualization experience and practice. The Power Shopper Visualization helps you recognize your Quality Guy. It will help you learn to see and recognize real qualities in a man and not only the flash, charm and attraction.

## Visualization:
## The Power Shopper

Take a deep breath.
You are ready to become a Power Shopper, so you can easily recognize the Quality Guy when he shows up.

Think about all of the wonderful qualities on your shopping list. These are the qualities that you want in a guy, the traits you admire and appreciate. Gently go through as many of the qualities as you can. You can also refer to your Shopping List, and just read them to yourself right now.

Take another slow deep breath and say to yourself, "I am open to recognizing a really great guy when I see him. I am open to recognizing when a guy is not a good partner for me. I am ready to be clear and aware."

Take another breath, and just imagine that a guy is coming to you in this vision. Can you see if he is a Quality Guy?
You can recognize the Good Clues, Bad Clues and know the Smart Shopper's tips. You know the Signs of Fabulous and Flawed that will help you make informed decisions.

Take another slow, deep breath and say, "I will use the clues and guidance of a Power Shopper to recognize my Quality Guy. I am happy to go shopping for a man and use my shopping skills."

Take a slow deep breath and SMILE.
Now you have what you need to go shopping for a man and recognize the Quality Guys who are right for you!

## Affirmation and Intention:
# THE POWER SHOPPER

Use this affirmation to recognize your Quality Guy. Try it right now. Claim your newfound abilities to know the clues and signs. You're becoming a Savvy Shopper. You are ready to use your skills to empower you to go *Shopping For A Man*.

Take a slow deep breath.
Smile and say,

**"I can recognize a Quality Guy when he comes into my life.
My Quality Guy is coming and I am ready to meet him
and see if he is right for me."**

Are you ready to go to the next levels of *Shopping For A Man*? Congratulations. Now, it's time to get a closer look.

CHAPTER
6

# GETTING A CLOSER LOOK
## A View Into WHO? Dates 2, 3, 4

You've compiled a great working shopping list and you began checking out the wonderful stores and outfits inside The Galactic Shopping Mall Of Love. You met, scoped him out and had your first date. Your first date gave you a lot of information. You got a closer look at the material, color, style and the relative fit of this garment. You know that this is not a deal yet. You're still checking it out. If you're still interested in him after your first date, then you are getting a closer look. That's why we're still looking at the problems and pitfalls. You need to know the deal breakers so you can increase your shopping powers.

Assume that your first date went well. Everything was great. It doesn't matter whether you were uncontrollably attracted to him. There had to be some chemistry or you wouldn't be going out with him. You are in observation mode. Watch and wait to see what develops. It's a skill you are learning.

The next three dates are browsing dates. You are just checking out the store, browsing, looking at the merchandise. Scan the store, let your impressions guide you, but you have not made any purchases. Your inner mantra at this point is, "Just looking" or "Just window shopping."

Dates two, three and four have the same rules as date one. Consideration is the key. If he breaks any of the first date rules in this early stage, rethink this man. He's supposed to be on his best behavior, impressing you with his charm, grace and attention. If he can't manage to do that three times in a row, there really is no hope. Think about it. You're still looking at the garment. You haven't really taken it off the rack yet. You're just thinking about it. Most times, you don't realize that when you are shopping, you are in control. You can just put it back on the shelf and find something else, something more appropriate to your needs and inner beauty. This is great. Remember you are in control in dating, too. You say yes or no. And when you practice these shopping tips, you will be thrilled at your results. No sense in wasting time in a store that doesn't have your style or quality. On to the next boutique!

*Smart shoppers listen!*
*A guy will tell you who he is, if you really listen to him.*
*He will show you who he is by his actions.*

Now, you can see deeper into his personality. You have an opportunity to look closer. If he's not willing to extend himself at this point, what will happen later? This may sound cold, but think about it.

You can't teach someone how to respect you. You can let someone know what you like. You can express your feelings, thoughts and reactions. It's his choice to respond appropriately. It's always up to him whether he wants to please you. If he doesn't, move to the next store and keep shopping. You never have to take home inferior goods and always, always check out the refund policy.

As you move into the next three dates, the conversation becomes more revealing. You begin to know more about this man. You discover some of his interests and personality traits. You know whether he gets upset if the waitperson brings cold food to the table. You know if he's a generous tipper. You know how often he thinks of you by how many telephone calls you receive between dates. You get all of this fascinating information by watching.

This isn't judgment. This is discernment. Everything you notice, everything he does, gives you insight, understanding and evidence for your shopping. You get to learn more about him and more about yourself. No fantasy. No projections into the future. No excuses for anyone's behavior.

Actions speak clearly. Watch what he's doing and how he's being with you. Conversation can only mask very certain actions, but the actions are always there. If he gets annoyed easily by what you do and expresses his anger, that tells you more about him than his continual apologies after the fact. He isn't showing you very much respect. If he's laid back and not much really annoys him, then you may see that you're very relaxed and at ease with this man.

Is he critical? Does he pick apart what you do or what you say? Does he correct your behavior? Does he tell you what to wear or what to order? He may do it with a look, a word or a sigh. This could mean that he doesn't give you much credit for your own opinions and life experience. It's good to know this. Shopping is getting to know him better and getting to fine tune what really works for you.

The clues are in bold print. Observe him. Pay attention to how he interacts with you. You have most of the clues you need to make very sound decisions on shopping for a man. You have your list and you can observe his behavior. I know this may not cover online dating, but face-to-face and person-to-person is where love becomes solidified. Everything is evident in the first three dates.

He is interacting with you and with others. Watch how he treats other people. Does he get along with most people? Does he berate them behind their backs? Does he have a positive attitude? Does he speak ill of his or your friends? Is he short tempered with others? Is he forgiving when the bartender spills a drink near him? Each action and reaction shows you what's going on in his life.

*"There has never been and
never will be another you.
You have a purpose - a very special gift
that only you can bring to the world."
Marie Forleo*

When you're shopping for a man, your first duty is to yourself. You're looking for a long-term relationship with a great guy who appreciates, respects and delights in you. You are fabulous and you deserve fabulous. Pay attention to his actions first. Watch what he does and how he does it. He is showing you the clues on the label. A person's actions are the most revealing. The conversations are second in line. Listen to what he says.

When someone tells you about their experiences in life, you can learn a lot about them. In a conversation about past relationships, listen to the stories of the lost loves and the reasons for their demise. Suppose he just told you about his ex-wife. She was so demanding in their relationship and expected him to provide things he just couldn't give her. He works very hard. He just wanted to relax and enjoy life when he got home. He didn't want to listen to her talk on and on about things. He didn't want to go out all of the time. The pressure and demands were just too much and it didn't work out.

Lots of times women first go to compassion. "Oh you poor, dear. It must have been awful." Think about it. What did she want? Would you consider it demanding? What couldn't he give her? Every one puts a slant on their stories to justify their actions. Put aside the exaggerations and get to the details. You don't have to pump him for this. You can just listen. This is great information about him and you need to know.

Did she expect him to work, do the housework, and raise the children with her? Sounds like she wanted a full partner. She could have been doing all of this herself. After all, she sounds like a wife. Did she want more of his time because he's so busy elsewhere? Maybe he committed more time and dedication to his career than to their marriage? Did he just come home, expect dinner, and give her and the family minimal time? Was he just too tired or inconsiderate to take her out or listen to how her day went? Did he take her for granted without sharing his life and his love? Did he make a mistake and cheat on her to get out of it?

He could be absolutely accurate in his description of their marriage. She may have wanted everything and not participated. He may have been really overworked and just wanted to relax and spend some time enjoying himself. This whole example isn't about judging him or judging his wife. It's about listening to what he is saying about living his life.

Don't judge him. Don't make excuses for him. It's not about that. Listen. He is revealing the clues about himself. He is telling you who he is by the story he relates. Think about what he means and what he says. You are shopping and he's revealing a lot of details to help you make your purchase or not.

Did he tell you that life was so hard that he cheated on her? I'm always very surprised when people are so forgiving about cheating, as though the circumstances justify the action. Some women actually feel that because he is sharing this, that he is baring his soul and that means he feels closer to her. It means if he confides in her that he is making a soulful connection. Really? If he's sharing about cheating, please be forewarned. He may be alerting you to expect the same from him. He might be saying that he'll rebel and leave if there's pressure there. Don't think that you can change a man who cheats on his wife. That's a rocky road, indeed. It's up to you to discover what's really being said, but in this situation, you have some very substantial clues.

I'm sharing different examples from many of my client's experiences, so you can scope out the store and see whether you want to shop there. When I'm consulting and coaching my clients about their soul purpose and spiritual growth, their relationships are always part of the consultation because it's part of their world. I can feel the good qualities and the flaws and gain a deep understanding about my client and their partner.

In this same way, I'm revealing some of the perils and pitfalls so you can see them and avoid them. I'm also revealing some of the fantastic aspects that you may not perceive, so you can be a successful power shopper.

What about this example? You mentioned that you're visiting your aunt. You tell him how close you are to your family. He says he's not close at all with his. Most children annoy him. His family is always prying into his life. As far as he's concerned, seeing his family on Thanksgiving and sending presents and cards is exactly how he likes it.

Are you listening? He doesn't enjoy being with family. If your idea of happy times is spending holidays and vacations with yours, you have heard his verdict. Do you want to give up your relationship with your family? He may not want any children around, his own or anyone else's. You always have your nieces and nephews visit for a week in the summer. You love them and you relish the time with your family. He just told you about himself. It would be to your advantage to listen. This is like an itchy wool sweater. You either like the scratchy feel or you avoid it at any price.

This is the exact situation my client Sarah had. She just started seeing a guy and through their conversations, he always avoided talking about children and family. She loves children. Everyone in her family has children and she took her nieces and nephews on fun excursions to sports games, parks and children's theater. On their third date, she asked him if he wanted children. He told her he wasn't the dad type. Instead of just letting it go, she was trying to figure out what to do. She was asking me what she could do to still date him, in hopes he would change his mind. I gave her my best advice.

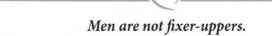

*Men are not fixer-uppers.*
*The only thing you can change about a man is his wardrobe.*

She got a closer look and he wasn't a good fit. It's not about changing a guy to suit what you want. That's the same energy as advisors telling you that you have to change to get the guy. So, she took my advice and just let it go. What's she doing now? She met a great guy who loves children. He even volunteers as a little league coach. That is more her style and fit.

Sometimes the clues are so clear, that you have to be in another world to misinterpret them. You're discussing relationships in general. He says that he has a hard time making long-term commitments. None of his relationships have lasted for more than a year, and he likes it that way. Maybe when he's older, he'll get married, but he doubts it. You just got your answer. This relationship is going to last a year at the most, and then he is going to walk. He just told you that.

Were you listening? He has already put a time limit on your relationship. So, are you thinking that you can change his mind and make him see the light of day? Why? He wants out before he's even in yet. No chance. Don't bother, unless you're willing to play around for a year and then find someone else. Understand that there are always exceptions to these rules. If he really is so fabulous that you can't think of life without him, take a chance. There are people who win big in the lottery. How many of them do you know personally?

In each of these situations, you have heard the truth about this person. When he tells you he isn't able to make a commitment, believe him. He's warning you not to get your hopes up. When he tells you that he just can't trust people to do the right thing, believe him. He can't trust you, either. When he says that he is a free spirit, accept the fact that he does not want to be in a committed relationship. If he says that the most important thing in his life is his work, just know that your relationship will rate under his career somewhere. If he says he is looking for the woman of his dreams and wants to fall in love and get married, then he may be your guy. He is telling you many of the things you want to know, before you even get involved.

**Smart shoppers listen!**

# SHOPPING POSSIBILITIES AND PERILS

These next few dates you are screening a man for his potential. These dates will help you decide whether you're going to take him off the rack. You're still far away from trying this one on. Relax, go to dinner and enjoy yourself.

There are situations you want to be clear about to avert any shopping perils. I mention several of the shopping perils throughout this book, but you may have hundreds in your own file system. The advantage of knowing the perils is knowing how to avoid them. A smart shopper has her list and she's sticking to it. She doesn't get side-tracked by some shiny little bauble displayed to distract her, so she forgets to get those great navy leather knee high boots. She has her list, she knows the qualities and attributes she needs for a great guy and she is ready.

You are in training to be a power shopper. Once you improve your skills, shopping for a man is easy. I believe in fate. I believe in destiny and I believe in the power of choice. Fate may bring you to the right place at the right time. Destiny may lead you to discover your truth and soul purpose. The power of choice brings you the wisdom, the opportunities to make your decisions based on your truth, your heart, your soul purpose and your vision. You are becoming a Power Shopper, fully informed and shopping for a man.

## Visualization and Affirmation:
# GETTING A CLOSER LOOK

Now, you're at a new level in your dating and shopping for a man. You know if there's any attraction. You had several dates and if he didn't seem right, you already know. You need a closer look, to see beyond first impressions and discover whether he has more qualities that delight and impress you.

You're becoming a Power Shopper and you're ready for a Closer Look. The next visualization and affirmation helps you see. It helps you get clearer and make decisions, without being dazzled by charm, good looks, or promises.

Begin this visualization with the "3 Steps To Centering" exercise. **The Closer Look Visualization** helps you recognize your Quality Guy. It will help you learn to see and recognize real qualities in a man and not only the flash, charm and attraction.

## Visualization:
## Getting A Closer Look

Take a deep breath.
You've had a few dates with someone. Now, you're giving this guy a closer look. You're more familiar with the qualities that you want in a guy, the traits you admire and appreciate. Now you're ready to see if this guy has and exhibits those qualities.

Take another slow deep breath and say to yourself,
"I can see clearly. I am taking a closer look to see if he is a Quality Guy and if he can be right for me. I have no judgment. I am ready to take a closer look and gain new perspective, right now."

Take another breath, and just imagine this particular guy.
Can you see if he is a Quality Guy? You can feel his energy, of course. Just go over some of the times you spent together and see how it feels to you. Did he respect you? Did he listen?

Take another slow, deep breath and say,
"I am taking a closer look to see if I want to spend more time with him. I can be clear and unattached in my decisions. What works for me is what is important, right now."

Take a slow deep breath and SMILE.
Now you have what you need to go shopping for a man and recognize the Quality Guys who are right for you!

## Affirmation and Intention: Getting A Closer Look

Use this affirmation to stay true to yourself and what is most important to you. Try it right now. You are shopping for a man. You want to be strong in who you are when you choose who will complement your life.

Take a slow deep breath.
Smile and say,

"I use my skills to take a closer look and distinguish a Quality Guy. I am happy to see the qualities and use my wisdom to make powerful choices in my life."

Congratulations. You're getting even more skill and practice in *Shopping For A Man*. Now it's time to see what you are buying.

CHAPTER

7

# WHAT ARE YOU BUYING?
## Going Through The Racks

You passed the fourth date. Congratulations. Everything is going right along. You're getting to know each other and you like what you see. You have your hand on the hanger. The jacket looks great. You've looked at the size, checked the tags and it seems great. It's passed the scanning mode and you feel ready to take it off of the rack.

List time! Take your shopping list out of its special place and read it. Go over each quality you have written and be totally honest with yourself. Is he really available? Does he have the qualities you feel are most important? Forget the romance and the desire. If you got this far, it's there.

This is a very pragmatic assessment. This list has nothing to do with fantasy. You worked very hard to discover what qualities, lifestyle and personality will complement you and support you in your life. You've gone through the closet and thrown away everything that outlived its time. Honor yourself and see if what you want is in this particular package.

It's time to discover what you really want and whether this guy fulfills those qualities. Sit down by yourself. Print several copies of your list and put his name on top of one. Check off every quality you think he has. The relationship is still very new. See what you think or feel about his qualities. Are you looking for someone who is romantic? Is he? Do you want a man who is stable and directed? Does he show signs of these attributes?

Take plenty of time. This is your first glimpse. You may not even remember everything you wrote on your list. Make sure you put his name on the top and start checking off the attributes. Put a star or a check mark next to every one that seems to fit. You are making notes on what he has shown you. You want proof of the quality. The dress on display looks like it's silk from across the room. You have to have some proof. The label has to say silk. It also has to say 100 percent silk.

If you are looking for a man who considers your needs, you must have explicit examples of his behavior. This is something that he did for you. This is not about what he said. Positive evidence is an action he took to show you he thinks about you, remembers what you said, and does something about it. Positive evidence is not displayed in words. It's not shown in assumptions or good feelings. Positive evidence is clear, recognizable, concrete action.

*You need positive evidence to decide if he's right for you.*
*He says it and he does it. That's evidence!*

# GATHERING EVIDENCE

All the details about your dates and what you notice are evidence. You simply notice and check everything that applies so you can recognize, remember and track the qualities that work for you. Again, it's not about judging the guy you're dating. It's being able to see and confirm if he is right for you. You are gathering evidence or seeing that you don't have evidence of the qualities you need in a man.

Your shopping list is your best friend. Print out a copy of your shopping list. Put his name on the top with the dates you went out together. I recommend that you start recording the evidence on date one.

# POSITIVE EVIDENCE

Here are some ways to recognize explicit examples of positive evidence. When you have real examples of positive evidence, place a check mark or a star and the date next to that quality or attribute.

### *ATTRIBUTE: CONSIDERATE*

**Example:** You had a bad cold, and he came over that night, cooked dinner and rented a movie for you both to watch.

**Example:** Your car was having some problems. He drove behind you to the mechanic, waited, and then drove you to work.

**Example:** You were waiting to find out whether you would get a raise. He calls you that night to find out the results.

**Example:** When you were together last, you mentioned how beautiful the irises were in the flower shop. The next date he arrives, irises in hand.

### *ATTRIBUTE: DEPENDABLE*

**Example:** He said he would call you to confirm your date at 6:00 PM, Wednesday night. The phone rang at six, on Wednesday. He called to make sure everything was all set for both of you.

**Example:** You told him you needed the name of an accountant to help you figure something out. He said he knew someone. He called you with the number the next day.

**Example:** You asked him to pick up a loaf of bread for dinner tonight. You forgot to buy it at the store. Right on time, with bread in hand, he's ready to help cook dinner.

Don't fudge this. This is not about a fantasy. Don't read meaning into something he said. You want reliable positive evidence. If he said something wonderful that's great. It just doesn't serve as an evidence of his qualities, at least, not yet. You want proof. No excuses from him or from you. His actions and follow through are the most important clues you have. If he said he was going to do something and he did it, that's proof. That is a clear example. If he said he would do something and he didn't, that's an important clue to watch. It's not what he said; it's what he did that proves it to you.

That's evidence.

Relax. You've only had a few dates. You don't have a lot of proof. That's the point. You're building a case for him. His merits will stand on their own. You're not judging him a good person or a bad one. If a dress is the wrong color for you, it's just the wrong color. It's not bad. It just doesn't work for you.

## NO EVIDENCE YET

Once you have the list of proven qualities and positive evidence, it's time to look at the "I don't know" category. You may not know if he is honest, yet. The circumstance hasn't presented itself. Go through the shopping list and put a question mark next to anything you don't know. You'll probably have more in this category right now, than any other. That's fine. Then you'll know what you don't know. If he's still intriguing, then you'll want to get to know him better. Remember, you must have a clear action for it to qualify as an example of evidence.

## NEGATIVE EVIDENCE

Finally, go through the list and mark each attribute that you know is missing. If you want a man who has a solid career, and your date hasn't worked steadily in two years, mark it down. Put an 'X' and the calendar date next to that quality on the list. If you listed a particular race or religion as your quality preference and he is another, mark it down. Very simple. This car model doesn't come as a hybrid. You want really great gas mileage and this one does have it, but it's not a hybrid. It may still remain on your list, but the features you want are not available on this model.

Some examples of negative evidence are easy to recognize. If you are a deeply spiritual woman looking for a deeply spiritual man, and he is not, this is obvious. This is negative evidence. Put a 'NO' or an 'X' next to that part of your list. If you have a certain financial status and want a man that equals or exceeds your income, a starving musician's income is a mismatch. So, that would be a 'NO' next to that quality or requirement. If you want to have children and he says he doesn't, it's clear something is missing. These all show negative evidence.

Jennifer is a very successful entrepreneur. She owns an alternative health and wellness company that she started. I coach and advise her in personal growth, increasing her business and fulfilling her life. She met a guy who was very creative and had a wonderful personality. He did have similar interests, especially in alternative health and spirituality. Sounded great, until she learned more. He didn't have a business or a steady gig. He was still exploring. He told her he still wasn't sure what he wanted to do for career or money, but he always managed to manifest the cash he needed. Jennifer loves her business, both helping people and being a financial success.

What did she ask me in our coaching session? She asked, "Am I being too limited? I want a partner who is also successful and excited about his work. Maybe I'm not giving him a chance? Is wanting a partner who is also successful stopping me from finding a great guy?"

I told her she was second guessing herself. She has negative evidence. She knows what she wants and needs in a life partner. Whether she felt guilty about being so successful or was too quick to compromise, she wasn't being true to herself. He can be a great guy and not be compatible, not be a great fit. Here's the mantra/quote I gave her to help clear the confusion and start shopping for a man.

*The features you want are not available on this model.*

All of this negative evidence is also great news. You are getting a clear understanding of who this man is because you can see which attributes he's missing. Now, you have a real choice, because you have a clear idea of who is there. If he told you he doesn't ever want to have children and you listed that you do, you need to think about this. You can choose not to have children. You can. If you can choose this without remorse, then fine. If you have always wanted children, he isn't right for you. When you are traveling to Chicago in the winter, you need a fully lined, really warm winter coat. Getting a cashmere scarf may help you along, but it's very cold there. There is a great chance of snow, too. You really need that coat. That scarf is not going to keep you toasty no matter how much layering you do. Making excuses means you are not comfortable asking for what you want and getting it. If you really want something, if you have goals, dreams and a knowing of what you want in your life and in your relationship, then please go for it.

Some examples of negative evidence are a little more cryptic. Let's say you listed a quality like compassion, intelligence or understanding. You have to find the clues in his actions or lack of them. Sometimes you have to look for subtleties. Don't be fooled by a glamorous package. The signs and evidence are right there.

## ATTRIBUTE: RELIABLE
**Example:** He said he would make reservations for dinner at 8:00. He picks you up right on time, but when you get to the restaurant there are no reservations.

**Example:** You told him you wanted to have a private little dinner at a cute new restaurant in town. It's all set. When he picks you up, he mentions that he invited a couple of friends to join you.

**Example:** You're meeting for lunch. He knows you have to get back to work at a certain time. He's late. This makes you late, because you waited for him.

**Example:** You found a really great business contact for him. You told this person all about him, and they are waiting to meet him. He never calls them, or calls them too late for anything to happen.

**Example:** He's going to fix your washing machine. He takes it apart and realizes he needs a new part. Four days later, no new part. He hasn't had time yet, and all of the parts are still on the floor.

These are examples that refute his reliability. That's all they are. You want reliable and he doesn't follow through there. This is negative evidence for reliability. It's a "NO" next to this quality.

## ATTRIBUTE: GENEROSITY
**Example:** You are out to dinner with some friends. The check comes. He figures out what you two have eaten. Reasonable. Then, he figures out his share of the tax and the tip. He doesn't want to give fifteen percent, and thinks ten is plenty, even though the service was fine.

**Example:** He's taken you out to a concert. You know the tickets cost a lot of money. You told him you're having a great time and thanked him. Several times during the evening he mentions how much money they cost him. He keeps on mentioning it.

**Example:** You're driving into the country for a picnic. You've packed a wonderful meal. You have a 4x4, so you pick him up. On the way home, you stop for gas. You pull out the wallet and pay for the gas. He doesn't offer to pay for it or split the cost.

These are situations where he could easily have been gracious. He wasn't. Generosity with money speaks a lot about a person. There are many ways that it can show up. In the first example, he could have split the dinner check right down the middle, unless the discrepancy between their meal and yours is considerable. It's not fair to split a bill when you had salad and they had full course meals.

You probably knew that those concert tickets were expensive. You told him how much you appreciate the concert and being with him. Reminding you of the expense shows that he's giving you something with strings attached. Not generous. He's waiting for a pay back of some sort.

Generosity has nothing to do with over-extending finances. Certain activities cost money. If he can't afford them, fine. It's his responsibility to pay attention to his income and make responsible decisions there. That's a positive attribute. If he reminds you about how much he's spent, or how much something cost him, then his giving is limited and it's negative evidence of generosity. He's not showing you that he is generous. There's no need to figure out why he's this way. That's for the psychiatrists. It doesn't matter why the manufacturer used cheap material on the dress. Who cares? If you can smell the polyester, then you know it's cheap. Are you going to buy it? I hope not. You are dealing with the facts. Generosity is on your list. He doesn't display this quality. It's vital that you know that right now.

All you are doing at this point is clarifying your statistics. Anything clearly missing from the list gets a "no." Cross it out. The "Great Galactic Shopping Mall Of Love" is a vast paradise of items. Shop for what you want. You have your list. Treat your shopping list as a valued friend, because it will show you what you are getting and how much it will cost you in time, energy, emotional satisfaction and investment.

After you finish going through every item on your list, you know better where you stand. If you crossed off or eliminated a substantial number of qualities, all that says is that he doesn't have them. It doesn't mean that he isn't a good person. It doesn't mean you are overly demanding. It means that there are certain things that you are looking for and he doesn't have them. Power Shoppers need to know if the store they are in actually has the items they want and need and that the store carries the quality that is best for them.

*"In any relationship each person should support the other; they should lift the other up."*
*Taylor Swift*

You created a list of qualities and traits that are meaningful for you. You need these qualities in a relationship. You want them to be there. Crossing things off the list shows you that those things that you feel are important are not qualities that he has or that he thinks are important. It's all very simple and to the point. If you crossed off a lot of things, you aren't getting what you want. This is early in your shopping for a man adventure. Remember this quote.

**If it isn't there, Buyer Beware.**

# UPGRADING YOUR SHOPPING LIST

It's important to upgrade your shopping list. When you first write your shopping list, you are looking at the most obvious traits that you want in a guy. It's a growing process. Your list not only reflects what you want in a guy, it also shows you what is important to you in your life.

## BAD SIGNS. DEMERITS. BONUS POINT

One part of upgrading is making notes about his actions. Tracking his Bad Signs, Demerits and Bonus Points keeps you on track. You'll know whether he is even better than you thought, or not. These qualities and actions may or may not be on your list. You may not be able to grade them with a 'YES' or 'NO,' but there is something that is not right about what he is doing or saying. That's why you should upgrade your list.

## BAD SIGNS

What's a bad sign? Bad signs are actions he took that didn't receive your applause. The quality this shows, may or may not be on your list, but there is something that is not right about it. You look across the store and see a beautiful cocktail dress. You may not need one right now, but it's so cute and you do tend to go out to events where one more great dress would make life easier. Everything about it looks great, but then you notice that a few of the beads are on the floor below the dress. These are signals of something you may not have on your list, but do not bode well for the future. The cocktail dress really wasn't on your list, and it's good to know that you don't have to get this one. The beads on the floor are a bad sign.

You notice him doing something that annoys you. It could be a habit he has of clearing his throat to get your attention. It may be that he takes extra sugars from the dispenser on the table in that cute diner. It may be that he isn't opening the car door for you, or doesn't call to thank you for the date. These all look like small things and most likely they don't show up as negative evidence on your shopping list. They are all still bad signs because they annoy you and you feel something negative, even if you can't put your finger on it right now. To be honest, I dated a great guy who showed a bad sign. It was a bad sign for me. Maybe someone else wouldn't even notice, but after a few dates it really annoyed me. It was never on my list until I started dating him. What was it? He chewed with his mouth open and made noise while he was eating. I know it might sound shallow, but it annoyed me too much. I'm using this example so you can see he didn't have a flaw. It wasn't negative evidence. There was nothing horrible about him. This was a Bad Sign for me. It was something I knew I could not overlook.

## DEMERITS

What's a demerit? A demerit is a subtle sign that something is off. If he said he was going to do something and then didn't, that goes on the list as well. It's a demerit. You may not have a particular quality in mind, but this doesn't sit right with you. You are learning about this particular man. Saying the right thing is all very well, but follow through is the proof that he means what he says. Talk does not qualify. Many people say things they don't mean or haven't considered. Some people even lie to get what they want. It doesn't matter why they do it. This garment loses points. Put a demerit sign, a D, next to the attribute. This is marked irregular. Irregulars are garments or merchandise with clearly labeled mistakes. They are still up for sale, but generally at a reduced price. Maybe no one else will notice it, but you did. It may never happen again. It may happen often. You don't know yet, so he gets a demerit. When you are shopping for a man, you're not looking for something shoddy. You want the best quality material you can find.

## BONUS POINTS

What's a bonus point? A bonus point is something lovely that he did that you didn't ask for or expect. It means he thought about you and what you would like, what would please you and then he did it. You mentioned you had a hard day and he cooked dinner for you. You told him about a concert everyone was raving about and he bought tickets. He sends you flowers just because he was thinking of you. These are all bonus points. These are extras that make life even more wonderful. Bonus points are thoughtful, considerate, caring and generous things he does for you, to show you he cares, he's paying attention and he can surprise and delight you. Cherish them. Add them to your list and mark them bonus points. Give this a big plus sign '+'. You want to remember the wonderful things that he does for you.

## EXPANDING YOUR SHOPPING LIST

Positive evidence, negative evidence, bad signs, demerits and bonus points are all different categories that show you very specifically what qualities this man has that are on your shopping list. They also reveal what you didn't put on your shopping list. That's important, too. Sometimes it takes a great guy to remind us of more qualities that we love and admire. Sometimes we need the demerits to remind us to pay attention to small opposing themes. That's what you need to know. Then you can add these to your list. Add the qualities you didn't realize were important. Notice what creates conflict or confusion for you.

These are not judgment calls on his character, his lifestyle or his capacity. You are shopping for a man and these particular qualities are important to you and either he shows that he has them or he doesn't. Oh, this makes dating so much more simple and fun.

### *I love shopping, don't you?*

Actions and evidence, that's what you are checking. He says it and he does it. That's proof of positive evidence. If he doesn't do what he said he would, there is something vital missing here. That is negative evidence. If his actions contradict his words, you better notice this now, or you could be looking at quite a few unfulfilled promises later.

This doesn't mean that you have to stop seeing him. It shows you who you are dating. If you are looking for happily-ever-after, he may not be the marriage prospect you want. You have fun together, so keep dating him if you like. It's okay. Enjoy his company. Good people are a pleasure. Life is filled with good people. Just remember that he doesn't have the qualities you need. Imagining him to be 'the one' will not serve you very well. The qualities he doesn't have right now, the 'no's' on your list, may be deal breakers in the future. That's what your shopping list is for, clarification.

Some women fall in love a lot. Each man becomes a prince in their eyes. No matter what qualities are lacking, he has potential. He may be married, but she's sure that he'll leave his wife for her. He may not want a commitment, but once he gets to know her, he'll change his mind. He may not have a job, but when they get more serious, he'll realize his responsibilities. Don't fantasize about changing him or creating him to be more of what you want.

It's perfectly fine to date this man and have a wonderful time with him. Just know yourself. Do you fall in love too easily? Do you latch onto the man who pays attention to you, even if you don't think he's right for you? Are you a serial monogamist? Do you date guys who end up hurting you? This man has signs of not being what you want. If you fall in love very often and too easily, stick to your list. Your list is there to help you. If this man lacks the qualities you need, be honest with yourself. Just go shopping and find one guy with the perfect fit to enhance your figure.

"You will never find what you are looking for in love, if you don't love yourself."
Lady Gaga

# Visualization and Affirmation:
# EVIDENCE AND AUTHENTICITY

You've had several dates and you have much more information about this guy. You've gone beyond what you think is quality and now you're checking the evidence to confirm that he has the qualities you admire and desire.

That's why we ask, "What are you buying?"

The next visualization and affirmation helps you see the evidence. Begin with the "3 Steps To Centering" exercise.

The **Evidence and Authenticity Visualization** helps you pay attention to the positive and negative evidence that shows you greater depths in this guy. You need to know, and the evidence is crucial. It's also important to keep your own authenticity. Be true to yourself. Be true to what you want and need. *Shopping For A Man* empowers you to grow more as a person. When you reflect on the qualities you have, the qualities and ideas that are important to you, then you can see more about yourself. If you still have some immature ideas or illusions about what will help you grow as a powerful woman in the world, then you can see it reflected on your shopping list. Great. You want to be more authentic to your core. If something is off with you, explore it and change it. If something is off with him, you have the evidence that will help you decide.

## Visualization:
## Evidence And Authenticity

Take a deep breath.
Now you're ready to see the evidence of qualities this guy reveals.

Take another slow deep breath and say to yourself,
"I can see and note the evidence from Quality Guy. The evidence shows me if how he is in the world and how he is with me is valuable and beneficial to me and to a relationship. Positive or Negative, I have no judgment. I am ready to see the evidence, right now."

Take another breath, and just imagine this particular guy.
Picture the evidence. See the examples of positive evidence. See the examples of negative evidence.

Take another slow, deep breath and say,
"Thank you for showing me the evidence that will help me."

Take another deep breath.
Think about what is important to you. Think about the vision and personal growth you want in your life.
You can see and recognize your own deeper levels.
Appreciate your own gifts, ideas and qualities.

Take a slow deep breath and SMILE.
You are more aware of your own authenticity. Coming from your own truth, you can see the evidence.
You are more aware, more clear and ready to shop and shine.

# Affirmation and Intention:
# Evidence And Authenticity Affirmation

Use this affirmation to stay true to yourself and what is most important to you. Your personal growth, your dreams and wisdom are very important. Your decisions about the evidence and whether or not a guy is right for you, starts with you. You decide. Try it right now. You are shopping for a man.

Take a slow deep breath.
Smile and say,

*"I recognize those qualities within me that I value and appreciate. I am learning to use my wisdom to make powerful choices in all areas of my life."*

*"I attract a quality guy that shows those qualities to me. I let go of anyone who does not value the qualities I appreciate and share."*

Congratulations. Knowing and making decisions based on evidence is key to *Shopping For A Man* and being the best you. Now it's time to Take It Off The Rack.

# OFF THE RACK AND INTO YOUR HANDS
## Reading the Labels

So far everything is going well in these first few dates. He continues to call and you continue to accept. He has shown some positive attributes and you like him. Is it time to take the dress off of the rack? 'Off The Rack' means that you want to see where this is really going and you already have some evidence that this guy is a good fit for you. Before you walk into that room with the little curtains and full-length mirrors, read the labels very carefully. Is it your size? What is the material? What are the care and washing instructions? Is this a designer label or a good manufacturer? Now comes a reality check. Are you going to get naked and try it on? Not until you read the labels!

Read the labels. You need to know the material and care instructions.

### EXAMPLE:
You have plans for your future. You want to get more education, start your own business and be creative. You're exploring new

things because you want to grow and learn in your life. You do want to have a solid guy, a monogamous, committed relationship that will lead to marriage. You know you're young, but you have dreams you want to fulfill. You want a quality guy who is happy to join the adventure and have adventures of his own.

He's a good guy. He's happy doing what he's doing. He smiles when you talk about your plans for the future and your dreams, but you know he doesn't really get it. He talks about his plans, but there's no passion and no future dreams. It's more about home and hanging with his buddies than it is about learning, exploring and making a difference in the world. He keeps mentioning that you don't know what you want yet, like that's a bad thing.

You can take this one off of the rack, but look at it closely before you head to the dressing room. Read the labels first. Check out those seams to make sure there's ample room to let them out a little, if needed. Hold it up to yourself first. Does the waist hit in the right place? Are the shoulders sitting perfectly next to your shoulders? This may look like it will fit, but on closer examination, maybe not.

### *EXAMPLE:*

You're really not interested in raising a family. Children are out of the question. You have a lot of friends, diverse interests and a great career. You want a marriage to share the excitement of life. You love to travel; you race cars and are very athletic. You are ready for a committed relationship with someone who is bright, articulate and adventurous.

He owns his own business and loves it. He was a downhill racer when he was younger and still goes to Europe to ski. He's been married before and his children are grown. He wants a partner to have fun with, bounce ideas off of, and share his hectic, rich life.

No problem with the children issue. He has his, they are low maintenance and you don't have to bear them or raise them. He is as interested in his work as you are in yours. That means he'll never question why you spend so much time there, and neither will you. You both love outdoor activities, so you'll have plenty of opportunities to spend time together. Both of your lives circulate around business, friends and action. If all goes well, you can each make a solid commitment to spend and schedule time together.

This size looks promising. The shoulders hang well. The proportions look great, even on the hanger. Take this one off of the rack. Be sure to check the inside seams and read all of the other labels. As far as size goes, this one could definitely work.

---

*"We are who we are, and when you accept people instead of trying to change them to fit your needs, your relationships can fully blossom."*
*Deepak Chopra*

# CHECKING THE LABEL FOR MATERIAL AND MANUFACTURER

Thank goodness for labels! All of the information is printed right there. There's no guesswork. The manufacturer's name is usually embroidered on the back of the neckline or the side panel. Just look inside and you will find who is behind this suit and its material.

You have your shopping list, so you know your purchasing criteria. It's not a judgment call whether a suit is wool, linen, silk, cotton or a blend of materials. That's a matter of taste. You are dealing with the question of quality. You can find cheaply made linen jackets and high quality synthetics. That's not the point. Look for quality in the materials. Then you know that it was made with care and assembled for maximum value.

Your potential purchase hinges on quality, value and dependability. You want to know if it will wear well and hold its shape. You want a product that's durable, from a reliable manufacturer, who stands by his goods and pays attention to its worth.

It's exactly the same in shopping for a man. It's important to know what he's made of and if he stands behind his agreements. You've come far enough to start checking his labels. This isn't an exploratory exam. Everything he does and says will show you what's on the label.

# LOOSE-KNIT OR TIGHT-WEAVE

### IS HE A LOOSE-KNIT GUY?

A loose-knit guy is easy going, but sometimes to a fault. Loosely knit garments usually get lots of snags with wear. They look great for a few wearings. It's a soft, casual, a relaxed look that gets noticed. Then your jewelry catches the sleeve. The button of your jacket pulls a thread in the front. Soon, every little outcropping of objects you walk by seems to attract another snag or pull, until the sweater is unpresentable.

The manufacturer knows that this is a great looking item, and has put that name right up front. This is for casual wear. It's cotton/silk blend that will look fresh and up to date this season. It's comfortable and relaxed. That's it. It's a great item for this season. There is no claim to it being anything else.

Who's this loose-knit guy? He looks and sounds great. You're attracted to his easy way of looking at life. He doesn't get ruffled when someone cancels an appointment. He isn't always on time, but he usually lets you know when he's running late. It really doesn't matter to him which movie you see, which restaurant you choose or if you meet on Thursday or Saturday night. He's easy, relaxed and comfortable.

Later, you're not really sure what he wants or thinks, because it really doesn't matter. The snags start to show themselves. Now, it seems he's non-committal and a little bit annoying. Why isn't it important to see you as often as possible? Why doesn't he care if you watch a love story or a murder mystery? What is going on in there?

There's nothing wrong with him, he just isn't a durable material. He sways with the wind because it's easier. It saves him from deciding what's important and going after it. Most of the decisions are going to be up to you. It's possible that the responsibilities will soon be yours. He may be totally available, honest and considerate. He could have many of the qualities you seek. The manufacturer makes no claims that this great sweater is going to be a staple item in your closet. It's loose and up to date. It hangs there for as long as it can, until there are some catches.

Maybe this man is perfect for a great season of fun. He could light up your life and bring you easy pleasure. He may even be exactly the type of man you want. You may thrive with this kind of guy. Are you willing to follow him around with a crochet hook, pulling in the snags for the rest of your life?

## IS HE A TIGHT-WEAVE GUY?

Tight-weave types are very dependable material. They can take a lot of wear. They hold up under scrutiny. You don't have to worry about your bracelet catching the sleeve. A little bit of dust will just brush right off. You can wear this sweater almost anywhere.

Class up a pair of jeans and a tee shirt with this sweater for a sophisticated and casual look. Dress it up with some smart accessories and you add unique pizzazz. Need a tailored look? It goes right into the office or meeting looking sharp, crisp and pulled together. It doesn't wrinkle up or look tacky even after years of wear. The manufacturer's label is embroidered inside the neck. It's a fine garment, with attention to detail and longevity.

The tight-weave guy looks and sounds great. He has very definite ideas about what he likes and where he enjoys himself. He is happy to share them with you and encourages you to do the same. He can show you off to your best advantage, because he knows quality when he sees it. He's comfortable with himself, so he can make his decisions and live with the results. He's on time because he said he would be. He's not pushy or controlling. He's confident in his skills and confident in yours. Anything that lies in the middle is open for discussion, and he'll listen.

Take this man off the rack and into the dressing room. You don't know if it's a fit, but it definitely has potential. He's not going to wrinkle at the first sign of a misunderstanding. He knows how to handle himself in a variety of situations. You can take him anywhere.

He knows what he's made of and is still flexible enough to explore new experiences. Generally there's no manufacturer's guarantee, but if it shows poor wear or is damaged in normal use, they'll stand behind their work. Quality goods are always the best bet. This one looks like he will wear well.

# CHECKING THE LABEL FOR CARE INSTRUCTIONS

Hand Wash, Dry Clean Only and Machine Washable are all different ways to care for your garments. It's best to know what kind of care instructions you and he need or require. There are no right or wrong instructions. It's all a matter of style. It's all a matter of what works best for you. You decide which level of care is right for your life style and you match your man to that. You may be a sensitive gal and want a man who appreciates that. You may have a high-powered life and want a man who can move quickly, think fast and assert his brilliance. You may want an easy, flexible guy and relationship. Even the words I just used in this description depend on what you think is easy. Easy for some is high maintenance for others. High maintenance for some is easy for others. The following care instructions can give you a good idea of what will help you keep your sparkle.

Guys come with labels. Check the care instructions to see if he's a hand wash, dry clean only or machine washable guy.

## CARE INSTRUCTIONS: Hand Wash

If you are a gentle, caring, nurturing person, you may not even notice you bought a hand wash item. You like taking care of good things. You're always there for your friends. You love to nurture. It's a pleasure. Making sure that his needs are met is a joy for you. It's not sacrifice. This is a hand wash only guy. You're being very well taken care of, too. There's always time to listen and to remember those little things that make him smile. You'll happily get out the gentle soap, spend a little time at the sink and take good care of that fine garment.

This is a man who wants your attention. He'll listen to you and expect the same consideration. You make sure he's taken care of because you love doing it. He's attentive and loving. He makes sure everything is just right for you. You'll cook dinner or he will. It doesn't matter as long as it's wonderful. If you both can't cook tonight, you dine out where the food is great and the atmosphere is comfortable. It doesn't have to be elegant as long as the two of you are together.

Attention is the key here. Hand wash only is the way to go, because you are both comfortable in this mode. He wants you to listen to every word he says. You need him to do the same. This is a man who needs time and wants to be the center of your life. Luckily, if he's good material, he'll make you the center of his life, too.

## CARE INSTRUCTIONS: Dry Clean Only

You're an on the go gal. You take care of everything that needs attention and care, but you don't have to do it all yourself. As long as you set the process in motion and make sure it's working, it will work well. You admire a dry clean only guy. You know that. He knows that. You're both comfortable with this arrangement. You share the responsibilities, they are precise and managed and that's the way you both like it.

This guy doesn't need moment-to-moment attention and care, and as long as it's done, you don't always have to be the one doing it. You arrange it. He likes being independent. He takes care of things in his life. You're not the homey type and you love things done very well. You work best with a dry clean only guy. You look to see if the garment needs cleaning. If it does, off it goes to the best dry cleaners to get the job done. When you pick it up, you make sure that every spot is removed, the seams are pressed right and it's in perfect condition. That's fine with him.

You don't have to cook the dinner every night, as long as it is well prepared, tastes great and on the table. You don't have to talk or text twenty times a day. If you have a problem, he'll support you. If you have things to do, he'll amuse himself. If you need his help, he'll give it, in his way, to the best of his abilities. If he can't do it, he'll find someone who can. He loves your expertise and is very comfortable with your style and power. He is proud of you and you both have similar goals, tastes and action levels. He wants things done well and running smoothly.

This kind of guy is dry clean only. He would rather spend more time with you than having you attend to the regular stuff in life. He has no concern about who gets things done. It's not about whether you cook dinner, make arrangements with your friends or take care of the details yourself. As long as things are handled well, he's happy and you are the same way. He's not a slacker and neither are you. Whether he does it, you do it, or you both find another way to get it done is just fine with him. Just make sure that it does get handled well. Then you can spend time together, have fun, get intense and share life.

## CARE INSTRUCTIONS: Machine Washable

You are doing the work, but at least you have some of the convenience. You can set some of this on relaxed mode. You know what he wants and he makes it easy for you to give it to him. You're comfortable with each other. This is a machine washable guy. As long as his needs are being met it's fine. He provides you with all of the tools for getting it done, and a little extra time is rewarded by an easy smile and cozy love.

You don't mind the extra time to hang up a few things along the way. He appreciates it. It's a little more casual because you both are relaxed. There's no rush. Everything gets done when it's needed. He helps out, because there's really no fuss to it. Cooking is easy. Good home cooking or gourmet dinners. It's all good. He knows how to cook some great basic dishes and will jump right in without asking if you're tired. He doesn't mind. He just likes your cooking better. If you both are too tired, either you have some lasagna frozen from the last batch you made, or you make something quick and nutritious.

Machine washable. Put the clothes in, wait, put them in the drier and then fold them up or hang them up. Relaxed. Easier than anything else because you don't have to go anywhere to get your needs met. Neither does he. He's honest, reliable and relaxed.

This is as close to chilled as you can get. Everything is very clear. You don't have to talk for hours to share your thoughts, sitting together, watching a sunset is fine with both of you. There's time for conversation, but it's generally loose. There are no real issues to discuss. You're both straightforward and uncomplicated. He lets you know what he thinks. If there are important decisions, you both talk and come to a working consensus and then take the actions already decided. If it needs reconsideration, you both take the next step.

There is a comfortable synchronicity between you both based on lots of qualities that are the same or complementary. Usually you talk about what's happened that day and you enjoy each other's company. The Machine Washable guy is not asleep or too laid back. He's present, but not manic or intense. Machine washable doesn't mean lazy. It's just more relaxed. He gets the work done and is really comfortable with who he is and what he needs to do and wants to do to have a great, loving relationship with you.

## CHOOSING CARE INSTRUCTIONS

There isn't any care situation that's better than another. Check out his label and see which care instructions apply. There is a dominant set of instructions and then a recessive set. You have one. He has one. The dominant set is how he usually cares for himself and how he expects care given. After the fourth date, the instructions are clear. They may not be printed in bold letters, but there is a definite pattern to maintaining his happiness.

He may be a dry clean only person. He's on the go and has his systems lined up to support his style. He breaks up his time in slots and knows when the car needs tuning, the bills are automatically paid and the important birthday presents are outlined on his calendar and purchased a week or more ahead of time. He has worked his life so that what needs to be done has a system to expedite it.

This is his dominant mode. During the weekends and on vacation, he relaxes. He'll pick up something quick to eat and he leaves a lot of open time just to hang out or go with the flow of life. During the weekends, he adjusts himself into machine wash. The main care instructions are still dry clean only. He's set it up so that when he wants to hang loose, the dry clean mode sets the scene so he can lapse into a machine wash setting for diversion.

Now that you have an idea of his care instructions, how do you find out which care instructions you follow in your life? This is all a matter of what works for you, how you like your life to flow and what you want to spend time doing. Since you are shopping for a man, it's good to know your own style so you can select what works best for you. It's likely you already know some of this. In relationships things change a little, so you can be flexible, but don't shift to the extreme to accommodate the guy, especially early in your dating.

*"In order to get what you want,
you must first decide what you want.
Most people really foul up at this crucial first step
because they simply can't see how it's possible to
get what they want,
so they don't even let themselves want it."*
*Jack Canfield*

# CARE INSTRUCTION CLUES

### *ARE YOU DRY CLEAN ONLY?*

How picky are you? Does everything have to be in your idea of order? Is timing and scheduling important to you? Are you very particular how your clothes look, your home? Do you plan ahead? Is your life jam packed with meetings, events and activities? You may be dry clean only.

This has nothing to do with finances. Being busy is a matter of choice. You approach life and set it up to maintain a certain level of accomplishment. You create other systems to expedite life for you, just in case. This happens in any wage scale or financial bracket. This happens whether you're in your teens or ready to retire. You would rather delegate the tasks at hand and see that they're accomplished. You don't want to pamper your mate or dote on him. That's too much. You want to be there to share the good times, support each other in the hard times, and work your life in your own way. You want to have a great, loving connection and create a fabulous life together, but you don't have to do it all. In fact you'd prefer to let the experts handle it.  Besides, you like those thin plastic bags shining over your newly pressed clothes.

A little note here, make sure you have a dry clean only guy or a guy who really delights in that method of care. If it doesn't work out, then after a little bit of moping, anger, confusion or disappointment, you will charge right out to find another. You have your detailed shopping list. Review it, make notes and go shopping.

### ARE YOU HAND WASH ONLY?

Hand wash is more hands on. Your main goal is the intimacy. Soaking those delicate garments in little pearly bubbles is a joy. You are comfortable with the extra care it takes to have something very fine and rich in your life. To outside appearances, you may or may not be living in luxury, but you create an aura of luxury around you. You have the time for long conversations. You take baths instead of showers, when time isn't pressing. The important thing is moments of quality.

You want to know everything about him. Sharing, growing, stretching the love is a key focus. You are happy and patient, knowing the process will unfold. You are more than willing to take the time to explore the realms of love with him. Your life appears looser, because you use time differently. There's a lot of flexibility in what you can do in an hour. You're just as particular as everyone else, but you do it in a different way. You like the idea of exploring the deepest realms of a relationship. If that silk crepe blouse has a little spot on the sleeve, you attend to it with care.

You're more introspective and sensitive. You have your shopping list, so make sure when you go into the dressing room that you're not considering a project. This is a relationship you are seeking. This is a guy, not a house renovation. Take a little time and review what works and what doesn't. You're patient and detail oriented, so this is simply part of shopping for a man.

### ARE YOU MACHINE WASHABLE?

You are practical, but are willing to go the distance. Whatever can be done quickly and well, you accomplish first. Then you attend to the details. You really want to whip through it, but you know some things take time. You just make sure that they don't take too much time and that there aren't a lot of them. You don't usually like to drop it into someone else's lap and wait for it to be accomplished. Too much lag time. You'd have to deal with their schedule and pick it up later. You are very hands on, but in an automatic, easy way.

You can attend to some of the details of hand wash and some of the efforts of dry-clean only, but you prefer a more relaxed life style. You check in with everyone to make sure they're okay, but unless they have a direct request, your time is generally limited. You like free time, and you don't always schedule an activity to fill it.

Your relationships are not generally dramatic. You have no patience for discovering all the intimate details or every possible motivation for every action in his life, unless they unfold gracefully. You do not probe.

Machine washable is in an easy-going, accomplishment mode. Everything is in your hands. It's all sorted. Whites and colors are separated and the load size is figured. You have containers of biodegradable detergent, good fabric softener and a small box of gentle suds for some of the delicate items that you can throw into the washer.

You like life to be comfortable and you work to make things run smoothly. You have a very flexible nature. What matters to you is if it's good. You have several pairs of adorable high heels in your closet for the required occasions, but you wear lower heels because they are comfortable. The criteria is whether it works well for you. You want a general sense of calm and fun.

Be aware. You may get stuck in fixing things in the relationship, but not out of the need to do it. You are competent, so it falls to you. You like to get in, get it done and get out. It's handled. You are nurturing, but more by what you do, than what you say. You're a machine washable gal and you can choose all these guys, since you're flexible and have the ability. So, just remember to grab your cute flats when you're shopping for a man.

*"When you're dating a man, you should always feel good. You shouldn't be in a relationship with somebody who doesn't make you completely happy and make you feel whole."*
*Michelle Obama*

## YOUR PREFERRED CARE INSTRUCTIONS

Notice which care instructions seem to fit you in an overall way. It's natural to flip into another mode when the occasion rises. There are times when we throw caution to the wind and put a silk shirt into the washer, anyway. It doesn't matter which category you fall into. Knowing which one you favor and which your date favors makes shopping easier. If you both have similar care requirements, you don't have too much to argue about. It's switching your care instructions that can give you a problem. You may be able to toss that silk shirt into the washer once. Continue to do it, and the shirt looses its luster.

If you're a dry clean only person and he's a machine washable guy, you may not be happy. He'll want more casual, home cooked food, while you're dreaming of that little Japanese restaurant that delivers Asian fusion sushi. He just wants a great pizza while you may dream of the hottest food trends. You want his needs met, but you are not going to be doing all of it. He wants you to be there. It doesn't matter what you're doing as long as you're there. You think it's more important to get it done well, even if it isn't you getting it done.

Compatibility is easier when both of you have the same or similar care instructions. If you switch any of these around, there's going to be adjustment. If you're a hand wash gal and he's dry clean only, you'll have some adapting to do. It's okay. That doesn't mean the relationship won't work. When you know yourself and you know his care instructions, you are ready and prepared to help things work. Luckily you are checking the labels.

Check the labels for the Materials, Manufacturer and Care Instructions. This is all part of Power Shopping. You have to read the labels to make sure you know what you're getting and what you're getting into. How can you really know what your label is? Look at your shopping list. You'll see your needs, preferences and wishes reflected there. You'll know how you are, how much care you need and what you want in a Quality Guy. How can you really know what his label is? Check your shopping list. That will give you the evidence you need. Listen to him. Pay attention to your time together. Checking the label is the best way to know what you're in for, what the general care requirements are and whether that will work for you. This may not be a deal breaker, but if you don't read the labels, or you ignore the signs, you may have problems.

*You're shopping. You have the power.*

# Visualization and Affirmation:
# IDENTIFY AND APPRECIATE

This visualization and affirmation helps you read more deeply into the patterns, qualities and lifestyle that you prefer and that your date prefers. Get into the focus of this the visualization with the "3 Steps To Centering" exercise.

The Identify and Appreciate Visualization helps you identify your own needs in a deeper and more practical way. You are seeing your own labels. It also helps you identify his labels, so you can see if your lifestyles are complements or a match. You're shopping for a man. You have to read the labels.

It's also important to appreciate yourself. Be true to yourself. *Shopping For A Man* empowers you to recognize and appreciate your life, your needs and your lifestyle. This is not a critical view. You are already fabulous. It's important to know yourself even deeper, so you can get what you want and what will complement your life, your dreams and a relationship. That's what your label shows. Give him that same appreciation. You may not be a match. His label may not complement yours. That's okay. It's all about shopping. Recognize the labels, and you have a much better opportunity to make great shopping and dating choices.

## Visualization:
## Identify And Appreciate

Take a deep breath.
Imagine that you can see your own care label. You know the quality of your material. You know the care you need. You already take care of yourself.

Imagine you can see Quality Guy's care label. You can see the maintenance he needs, how much attention or how little attention he wants and you know the quality of the materials. You have a good sense of this, just by what you've noticed about him.

Take another slow deep breath and say to yourself,
"I can Identify and Appreciate my labels for Materials, Manufacturer and Care Instructions.
I appreciate myself for where I am right now in my life."

Take another slow, deep breath and say,
"I can Identify and Appreciate the labels, for Materials, Manufacturer and Care Instructions for a Quality Guy."

"I have no judgment. I am ready to see whether our lifestyles, goals and dreams are compatible, right now."

Take another deep breath.
Tune into yourself and then tune into him.
Whatever you see or feel right now, is guidance for your dating and shopping. Is this a good fit? How does his lifestyle and energy feel with yours? You can see and recognize your own deeper levels. Appreciate your own gifts, ideas and qualities.

Take a slow deep breath and SMILE. Now, you're more aware of the lifestyle and priorities for each of you. You are ready to take it to the next level or go back for more shopping. Either way, you have a true appreciate for your self.

## Affirmation and Intention:
## Identify And Appreciate Affirmation

Use this affirmation to stay true to yourself and appreciate what is most important to you. Sometimes you may be too critical of yourself when things don't go your way. Appreciate your core beliefs. Your dreams, talents, gifts and wisdom are very important. Love yourself.

Take a slow deep breath.
Smile and say,

*"I identify and appreciate my qualities as a woman.*
*I appreciate my self and my life."*
*"I attract a genuine, quality guy whose character, values*
*and lifestyle I can appreciate and enjoy."*

Congratulations. You Took It Off The Rack and read the labels. This is key to Power Shopping. This is the next step in *Shopping For A Man*. Now, it's time to go to The Dressing Room.

CHAPTER

9

# THE DRESSING ROOM
## 3 Criteria for a Fantastic Fit

Finally, you're on your way to the dressing room. It's time to get naked and try it on for real. All of the time you spent busting the illusions, cleaning the closets, making your shopping list and checking the labels has paid off. Dating technically occurs after five or more consecutive dates. Anything before date five is considered checking the list. So, you checked the list. That means, he seems appropriate and you really like each other. It's date five, so now you can actually consider yourself dating. Taking the garment to the dressing room equals dating.

So far, so good. Now the real fun begins. You're in the dressing room. Pull that garment from the hanger and slip it on. Well, how does it look? Don't really know? That's where the criteria for a great fit come into play.

*When you are shopping for a man, the three shopping criteria apply. Make sure he's a good fit, he enhances your true colors and he complements your personal style.*

# CRITERIA ONE: A GREAT FIT

First things first. Criteria One is about A Great Fit. You are looking for a great fit both with this man and in a relationship. That's primary. The man you are dating and the relationship you are creating are like a dress. When you slip this dress on, it should glide on easily. If you have to pull and tug it, just say, 'no'. If it swims on you, if it has issues, like bad seams or an odd fit, this one goes back. Don't bother imagining different ways to fix it up. It's too early to think about alterations. If you can't get into it easily, just forget it. Get dressed and send it back to the rack. No sense wasting precious shopping time. He's the wrong guy.

## *SHOULDER FIT*

There are definite criteria for a good fit. The shoulders are important so they should lie comfortably and appear aligned and squared, so the garment falls gracefully from there. If one shoulder comes forward and the other back, that dress will never look right. If it doesn't look good now, you may never take it out of the closet later. It's the same with a man. If you aren't comfortable with how he is when you are out together now, you may never take him out of the closet.

Look at the little things. If the shoulder pads are too large for you, that can be changed. The shoulder pads are a minor detail. The cut of the shoulders is major. In a dress, a suit or a man, the shoulders are what hold everything up. If the shoulders are off or they slump, there's no stability. You don't want to adjust something major. Shoulders are major. If he is weak and complaining, if he changes his mind all of the time, if he is too tight or too loose at the shoulders, try another one. Put him back on the rack. Shoulders are about stability, strength and poise. You want stability in a long-term relationship. If it's not there now, just march back to the rack and start browsing again. What you do want is a graceful flow from a strong balanced shoulder. They should carry the weight of the garment with ease and style. If the shoulders don't fit or line up well, don't worry; there are thousands of items to choose from. If the shoulders are fine, you can check the next area of fit.

## ARM AND SLEEVES FIT

Arms and sleeves are the next area of importance to your fit. If you want freedom of movement, look for ample room under the arms and in the back. You want to be yourself. The dress or man is there to add to your life. If you feel restriction, it doesn't pay to buy it.

Remember: anything or anyone that holds you back is no bargain. You want to move in this relationship. You want room to expand your experience, your love and your ideas. If the suit jacket is too tight in the arms or the back, your relationship is already confined. It's cramping your style.

If there is too much room under the arms, the jacket doesn't fit either. It starts to look haphazard. It's almost droopy. You want to move in it, but you also want some structure. You want a committed, long-term relationship. If it's really too big for you, if the guy is too loose, if there is no definition at all, you'll get lost. You won't know whether you're heading towards a relationship or out of one.

Pay attention to this area, too. You are still shopping and right now it's not about alterations. It's about whether you even have a fit.

## FRONT FIT

The front of the garment is what you see first when you look in the mirror. The front of the dress or jacket shows you off. How does it lay? Are the buttons popping or pulling because they're too tight? If they are, then you are restrained. If you choose this model you are limiting your expression. You won't be able to come forward because you'll be too guarded. It's too tight and this means you can already see that this guy is a bit too tight and binding. You will be afraid to speak your mind or stand your ground because there are already too many rules, regulations and guidelines. Good to know and to see it now.

Is the front of the garment too loose? There's not enough closeness. You want room to move, but not so much room that you seem to be reaching across a cavern to make personal contact. You get to decide how much room is freedom and how much is intentional distance. You want to grow and learn with this man in your life. You don't want to have to use a GPS to find him when you need him.

## WAISTLINE

Now, look at the waistline. It's called a waistline because it sits just about on your waist. This is your satisfaction level. You're not going to know yet if you will be fully satisfied in this relationship, but you want to know that it's possible. If the waistline doesn't even sit right at this point, it's already too much work to bother. A long-term relationship will give you hundreds of things to work on, so why have to work at it after only four or five dates?

Check whether the waist is too loose or too tight. If the waist is too tight, you're squeezing yourself into it. This means that you are trying to hold everything in, just so you can have the outfit, just so you can have the man. It's not going to do you any good later. You want to share yourself. You want to breathe your life. If the waist is too tight now, then the guy will be too tight for you. He'll be too restricting or judgmental and you won't feel free or fulfilled. If it's too confining right now, this may be a very rigid relationship. Imagine sitting in a dress that is too tight. You're out to dinner and the waist is too tight. This is even before you actually eat. Feel all of the ways you have to move so it still looks good, and it doesn't stretch. Do you really want to unbutton the waistband now? Are you afraid the stitching may rip? If that's a relationship, where's the fun?

If the waistline is too loose, then it hangs all wrong. This is a mismatch. You want some room there, but not so much room that when you belt it, or button it, you look like you're wearing someone else's clothes. You are creating your own life. You are choosing a man who is right for you. Give yourself credit for knowing what you really want and what 'suits' you. This just may not be your size or the designer may have someone else in mind. Everything about it has to be smooth, well proportioned and comfortable. You're just beginning to date and this is not the time for reconstruction or accepting a poor, tight fit.

## COLLAR

Next, look at the collar. It must all lay flat. The collar is an extension of the shoulders, and if this is off the whole garment can look a little sloppy. An ill-fitting or ill-constructed collar throws everything off. This is how he pays attention to you. His responses are like the collar. Any assembly problems will hurt the whole line and structure. It may appear to be a detail, but it's very important. If the collar pulls forward or back, you will look and feel off-center. You will constantly adjust yourself to balance the jacket. You will be trying to adjust your inner self to his emotional needs and how he reacts. He may be too demanding or jealous. He may be showing signs of telling you how to think or feel. He may be the opposite and not really notice what's important to you because he's a bit askew. No good. You don't want to pull and tug at yourself for twenty years in a relationship. You don't want to pull and tug at him, either. You are looking for a smooth fit.

## MINOR ALTERATIONS

The shoulder pads, sleeve length and the hemline are the only places you can have some leeway in the dressing room today. The shoulder pads can be removed. You can change the shape of the shoulder pads and alter the shoulder line slightly, but not rework the whole shoulder of the garment. If they are a little long, you can deal with it and have them altered to fit. The hem can be raised or lowered to the desired length. The shoulder pads, sleeves length and the hemline stand for your flexibility in the relationship. If there is ample material to lower a hem, you have room to speak your mind. If you can shorten the sleeves, you know you and he can work on things together. If you want to change the shoulder pads, you know you can continue to update your relationship as it develops. This gives you some flexibility.

The shoulder pads, sleeve length and the hemline are areas of minor alterations. You are not changing yourself to fit into the relationship. You don't have to diet to look great. You don't have to change him to suit your needs. You don't have to change yourself to be loved and appreciated. You look great, feel great and have some comfortable room to move. Changing the hemline or adding different buttons are the little things you can do because you're an individual. These are requests, they are areas where you and he can accommodate some shifts. Real partnership embraces minor alterations.

With a quality garment you have some opportunities for alterations. No one is perfect. You may need to move a shoulder pad slightly to have it fall just right. That's a simple alteration. If it doesn't fit perfectly, but is exceptionally close, this garment can take some tailoring without any stress. If you have to take off the sleeves and reset them, you're remaking the jacket. You're trying to remake the man to fit you. Put your credit cards away and forget it.

Shopping for a man is so much fun. You are completely unattached to this dress or suit. You are finally trying it on, just to see if it will work in your life. You are looking for something great and you're going to find it. Don't be discouraged if it doesn't float onto you like the gown the Fairy Godmother made for Cinderella. She couldn't go shopping. Cinderella was too busy dealing with a whole lot of ashes. Luckily, she had the right shoes!

# CRITERIA TWO: TRUE COLORS

Everything is going along well in the sacred cubicle of fashion, the dressing room. Now you can delve into Criteria Two, the True Colors. When you are shopping for a man, the color has to be flattering to you. The color makes you look great. How do you know if he is the right shade of blue for you? Your skin tones glisten. Your face is warm and inviting. The color enhances your eyes, your hair and your image. Criteria Two, the True Colors, equals his tone and attitude. Choosing a man by the right color for you is looking at his tone in life. His attitude and way of being has to complement you. A brash, bold man may complement a quiet, reserved woman. Then again, he may overshadow her.

If he's a brilliant red, he is bold, daring and adventurous. He's definitely a risk taker. He's out to have fun and to be noticed. He likes to be front and center. It's where he thrives and where he belongs. People remember him. You may be used to burgundy, grey and navy men. They're strong colors, too. They simply tend to be more conservative, more thoughtful and introspective, but their main stance is controlled power. They are the classics, tried and true. You know what to expect from them, especially if you're used to dating them. A brighter red may be just what you need to perk up your life.

A man in the brown shades is earthy, warm and grounded. In all of those tones of brown, from tan and taupe, to cocoa and sienna, to chocolate and umber are a variety of interesting traits. There's a soft warmth to this man. He is solid. He is reliable. He will stand by you. You may be attracted to beige, because it's soft, warm and very classic. It complements most colors, from dark blues to blacks, reds and browns. A man whose True Colors are in the brown tones is very adaptable. He's not pretentious, but he knows his worth. He mixes with some of the brighter colors and can be a solid complement to your life.

Every shade has its saturation and blend. Purple is a blend of red and blue. So a man whose True Colors go to purple has the boldness of red, but the reliability of blue. Purple is deeper in saturation, with a deeper, redder color in it. These colors are all descriptions of men. I know there may be stereotypes about colors. Forget them. You are shopping for the color that looks great on you and complements your life. You know what colors you look good in, but such a vast selection can leave you dazzled and bewildered. Remind yourself that you are looking for the True Colors, the man that lifts you out of the crowd and flatters your life.

You want to shine. You want your eyes to sparkle. You want your complexion to radiate. Color will do this. You decide which color and how much of it is the best blend for you. That orange man may be the life of the party. He dazzles everyone. He is fun, entertaining and witty. You saw him across a crowded mall and your eyes met. The display was upbeat, unusual and absolutely fascinating. You tingled with delight.

In the dressing room, you discover whether that clever, vivacious man is complementary to your personality and lifestyle. Are you a gal who can carry off orange? You'll definitely be noticed. Does the orange man give you the lift and energy you've always wanted? Does he brighten your life? Does he boost the richness of your dark brown hair? Or does he overshadow your delicate complexion? Do you look washed out and pale? When you are with him, do you fall into the background? Is he the only one who gets any attention? Does he end up making your skin look red, blotchy and uneven? All these descriptions are the color choices you make in choosing a man.

Don't worry about the colors you usually select. For one reason or another, these comfortable color choices haven't worked yet. You don't have that perfect item happily tucked away in your bedroom to have and to hold. You may need more sparkle in your life. This guy could just be a bit too boring and conservative for you now. Choose someone brighter, deeper or richer than you're used to buying.

Maybe you always toss the brightest colors into your shopping bag. Brilliant reds, oranges, lime green. It might be time to subdue those colors. Maybe he's fun and exciting for a while and then it gets a little dated. He could be the hot color this year, and next year he's definitely passé. Maybe he requires too much attention and doesn't have enough substance.

Shopping for a man is a skill. In the dressing room you hone your craft. You expertly try on each item and decide whether it's worthy of your money and your time. It has to flatter you. That dress must look wonderful on you. It has to bring out your finest attributes. You are shopping for a man. The man you choose has to enhance your life. The color of him, his particular tone and attitude, can improve your existing qualities. It can boost a reserved nature or tone down a flashy one. It can bring energy and excitement or quiet gentleness into your life. It's your choice.

Color is one area where you can be a little daring, if it looks great. Of course the color has to complement you and the rest of your wardrobe. That's a given. Everyone has favorite colors. It becomes a comfort zone. Expanding your repertoire may be just the twist that gives this man the bonus factor of lighting up your life and enhancing your complexion. Right now, you're just trying it on.

*"Personal Style comes from within. It's when the woman, her individuality and spirit come through."*
*Donna Karan*

# CRITERIA THREE: PERSONAL STYLE

The dress fits. The jacket is the perfect color complement. What about the style? Is this the latest fashion creation? Is this a contemporary classic? Are you street chic, elegant or more haute hippy eclectic? Does this dress have enough flair to lift you out of the doldrums the minute you wear it? What's the cut of the outfit? Does it have a lot of detail? Is there top stitching? Does it have little buttons running down the front or a zipper in the back? Is it lined?

Style is a matter of taste. You know what you're shopping for, and you know your own taste. At first glance, style consists of how you see yourself. When you look at yourself in the mirror, you pick out certain features that you choose to project. It may be your eyes, your figure or your hair. You have a flair for certain clothing. You relate to the world in your own way. You see the world through your own vision and you extend this into the world.

Your personality is just like fashion. After the clothes, who you are is what you communicate. Criteria Three is about your Personal Style and his Personal Style and whether they're a good fit. Many women choose a style of a man that is different but complements their own personality, their own Personal Style. It's important to discover and choose what you are comfortable with, what you're striving for, and what complements all of your inner qualities.

Personal Style is how you like to do life. Your lifestyle may be casual. You're not obsessed by cleaning the house or the perfect table setting. Inside you may be a perfectionist with how you relate to people. You may be very careful about what you say and how you say it, so you don't offend anyone. You may be jeans and a great sweater, normally, then impeccably tailored clothes for going out.

Your style may be dress-up elegant with pop of pizzazz. Designer labels, even if they're on sale, are for you. Every outfit has its mode and ambiance. You may blend your life to meet all occasions, from lots of dressy parties to days at the beach. Your Personal Style may be all business. You may be all home life. You could be the leather jacket, edgy style. There are so many styles and flavors to all of us. It makes this a rich and exciting world. It's impossible to list all of the fabulous examples of personal style.

*"Find someone who wants an equal partner.
Someone who thinks women should be smart,
opinionated and ambitious. Someone who values
fairness and expects or, even better, wants to do
his share in the home. These men exist and,
trust me, over time, nothing is sexier."*
*Sheryl Sandberg*

This is where you know you. When you wrote your shopping list, you started to understand your style in the world. By selecting the qualities for your man, you've outlined your own Personal Style. You chose all of the clothes and accessories for your perfect wardrobe. These are the attributes that you hold important. These are the attributes, the qualities in this world and in a guy that you admire, respect and are not ready to compromise. You know that they complement you and enhance your life. All of these qualities are a partial description of your own style. That's why you appreciate them.

How do you find out more about your personal style? Ask yourself, "Who are you? What style of living do you prefer?" Be honest with yourself. You know how you relate in the world. You know what your comfort level is and you know what you want.

The garment is off the rack and in the dressing room. So far, this guy looks very good, or you wouldn't have draped him over your arm, brought him to the dressing room and tried him on. Does his style match or complement you? Really look at it.

Your style doesn't have to match your care instructions. You may be a Hand Wash Only person in your relationships, but very loose in how you do your life. When you can see your own personal style of living, you have a better chance of seeing who is comfortable playing with you.

Don't be afraid to try out new things. You may be in a shopping rut, just buying what you know, and it hasn't worked. Your style doesn't have to be rigid. It's what you know about yourself right now. You can be flexible. Just make sure that you don't stretch yourself to the limits to accommodate a man. If you're flexible, you want him to be flexible.

Ask yourself how does this one measures up? You have a good idea of what you want. Quality items have tight, even stitching. All of those little threads are matched. No big knots, no back stitching to cover up a seam, no loose threads. The seams of a garment hold everything together. With a high quality garment and a high quality man there are no puckered seams hiding in the interior of the garment. When you're shopping for a man, you want one that will still be great on days you're bloated and days when you're thinnest. You aren't shopping for 'special occasions only.' You want a style that complements your life, that allows you to be yourself and still works every time.

Style is another area with leeway, creativity and flexibility. Once you know your own way of being, you can choose someone who complements you, adds to your life. He doesn't have to duplicate everything that you hold dear. You want a bit of sparkle there. You don't have to get stuck picking the same style every time. Give yourself a break. You can go for something with a little more pizzazz, without going overboard. You can add some edge without being hard core. You can start to buy contemporary classics, if you have always followed the hottest fashion trend.

You want to look great, feel divine and be yourself with confidence. Any style that overpowers or overshadows you will be your demise. If he's an overpowering style of man, he will continually need attention. He may always overshadow you so that you defer to him or you cater to him. You may have to press him before each wearing. You may continually adjust yourself all night so the fabric lays smooth and the lines stay just perfect. He just may be too buttoned up for you.

Any style that requires too much maintenance while you're in it is a nuisance. This means that you have to pay attention to him and how he's doing. Naturally you want to pay attention to him, but not all of the time or an overly amount of time. You could end up spending more time adjusting yourself to him than being complemented by him. It just won't work as well as you hoped. This will end up being more trouble than it's worth.

Don't sacrifice comfort and value for style. Just because everyone is enamored by this impeccable coat, doesn't mean it's right for you. You want a man who makes you feel great. This isn't idle flattery. This is impeccability. He puts you in your best light without overshadowing you. He boosts your world into a better place to live. He knows who you are and loves you.

Right now you're still in the dressing room. If the coat is awkward, you won't feel great later. If the dress is not the right personal style for you, if it doesn't help you look and feel great and complement your life, then just leave it in the dressing room and continue shopping.

Is the style appropriate? Do you think it will really work with your wardrobe? Can you wear it with most everything? You're not looking for a rhinestone necklace. You want the pair of 18 karat gold earrings that are always in style and always bring that quality sparkle into your life. You want the wide antique silver bracelet with a unique design that has the feel of quality and while it gets attention, you're the one they notice. You want the handmade ring by the artist who mixes the most perfect precious stones in his settings. This is the ring that shows off your own personality and still shines with its own individuality and excellent craftsmanship.

Style is important because it dictates the basic lines. Too much style will overpower you. Not enough style will leave you flat. There is plenty of room to play here, because style can fluctuate. This is where you can be flexible, but don't sacrifice who you are for a guy. You're still shopping for a man. If the lines work with you, the buttons can always be changed later. If it needs a little punch to boost its appeal, you can be creative with accessories. But if the style doesn't bring out your best attributes and enhance your life, no amount of scarves, brooches, wrappings and trappings are going to pull it off. If this guy doesn't complement your life, help you shine and bring you joy, freedom and extra goodies, then he stays in the dressing room and you move on.

If he isn't really what you had in mind, if your styles collide, hang it up and start again. Have no attachment to the process of shopping. There's so much out there, selection can be confusing. You are clarifying your choices. With each adventure shopping for a man, you'll notice that you are getting closer and closer to what you really want. Your skills get so much better. So, put your clothes back on. Comb your hair and touch up your lipstick. Try the next store. You know, it's that little boutique across the way that has those handmade clothes from the local designers.

Now, if this little number satisfies all of the standards, complements your life and you think it will help you stay fabulous, you are ready to buy. The cashier is hoping that everything is perfect for you. She is waiting to make your purchase as easy as possible. Cash? Check? Credit card? It's all up to you. She's going to wrap it up and send you out into the world with a smile on your face.

*"You do not need to be different from who you are. You only need to be more of the person you already are."*
*Brian Tracy*

# Visualization and Affirmation
# THE GREAT FIT

This visualization and affirmation helps you read more deeply into the patterns, qualities and lifestyle that you prefer and your date prefers. Begin with the "3 Steps To Centering" exercise.

The Great Fit Visualization helps you know what is a good fit for your soul and your life. It all starts with you. You want to know what really fits for your own needs and for your relationship. You're shopping for a man. He has to fit or it's not going to work.

One aspect of a Great Fit is being comfortable in your own skin. You know your quality, style and true colors. Yes, you can grow and evolve. Knowing yourself is important. *Shopping For A Man* empowers you to appreciate your life and discover the qualities, ideals and connections that will really complement your life. You will have a great fit when you know and appreciate yourself, take into account what fits for you, and you make great shopping choices. It's all about shopping. A great fit is vital.

## Visualization:
## The Great Fit

Take a deep breath. Imagine that you have a whole new under-standing of yourself. You can see your growth and you know what's really important to you. You know that to be happy in a relationship, you have to honor yourself.

Take another slow deep breath and say to yourself,
"I honor and appreciate myself for where I am right now in my life."

Take another slow, deep breath and say,
"I attract a Quality Guy who is a Great Fit in my life, right now."

Take another deep breath and say,
"I am comfortable with myself and what I need. I trust myself to know what is best for me in relationships and life. I do not need to change myself just to attract or keep a guy. I am blessed."

Take a slow deep breath and SMILE.
You are more aware of a deeper part of yourself. You know that the Quality Guy will come and he will be delighted and excited to be with you.

## Affirmation and Intention: The Great Fit Affirmation

Use this affirmation to stay true to yourself and appreciate what is most important to you. Sometimes you may be too critical of yourself when things don't go your way. Sometimes you may give in too quickly. Appreciate your core beliefs. Your dreams, talents, gifts and wisdom are very important. Love yourself.

Take a slow deep breath.
Smile and say,

"I trust myself as a woman. My values, qualities, ideas and dreams
are beautiful."
"I attract a genuine, quality guy who is a great fit for my soul and
my life."

Congratulations. You Took it Off The Rack and read the labels. This is key to Power Shopping. This is the next step in *Shopping For A Man*. Now it's time to find out if it's a deal or an ordeal.

**Quick. Get dressed. There's no line at the register.**

# ODE FOR THE DRESSING ROOM

Is it worth the money dear?
Can you wear it there and here?
Can you wear it to the store?
Will you wear it more and more?

Can you bring it to a wedding?
To the board that you are heading?
Does it show your style and flair?
Does it complement your hair?

When you wear it, does it please?
And your longings, it appease?
Of your praises does it sing?
Does it go with everything?

When you put it on for size
Does it move and tantalize?
Does it show you to your best?
Putting you above the rest?

Will it soothe and ease your mind?
Leaving others well behind?
Do you look and feel divine?
Will it stand the test of time?

Is the value tried and true?
Giving more and more to you?
If the quality is beyond the pale
Tell the cashier, "Ring up this sale!

CHAPTER
10

# IT'S A DEAL!
## Taking It Home

Finally. The cashier is in full view. She's smiling at you. You're ready to take this baby home. You have examined everything that you can in the store. It all seems perfect. You know that you have the money for this purchase. It's time to buy it. It's a deal. You think it's a deal. You're finally taking it home. It doesn't matter which method of payment you choose, as long as you can return it.

A deal is serious dating. You are taking him home. You bought this fantastic garment and now you can really see how it complements you and if it will wear well. You hope that this is a keeper. You hope that this will grace your life for a very long time.

First, make sure that you can return your purchase. The excitement and thrill of finding a good one and taking him home can put the best shoppers in a daze. Try it on again at home. Don't take the tags off yet. This will help you decide whether you keep this one. You want time to see it in your own light. Store lighting can be glaring and distracting. Then see if it really does go with those brown snakeskin shoes. You will know if the shade complements your favorite suit. If not, at least you have the receipt.

Being able to return your purchase means that there are no strings attached yet. There is no commitment. You have no plans of marriage. You do not share the same bank account. He is not added to your credit card. You are not living together. You're not buying a home, boat or car together. You are not having a child with him. If you change your mind, at any time, you can go merrily back to the mall and return him.

Beware of 'final sale only' signs. You may be courting a bit of trouble. A final sale happens when there are certain reasons or deadlines in finding a man. He gives you an ultimatum, a put up or shut up scenario. It may be as simple as, 'If you loved me, you'd... move in with me... have sex with me... let me borrow some money...'.

It could also be more extreme. He may get thrown out of his apartment and have to live with you. Guess what? He doesn't have to live with you. If he says that, you're already in trouble. If he needs cash right away because something horrible happened, stand clear. Where are all of his friends and family? This is very early in a relationship to make demands or requests.

Don't be pushed into a deal. Right now the tags are still on the garment, you have the receipt and the bag. Beware of overt conditions that speed you into a commitment. These situations can be his or yours. High-pressured sales can confuse your judgment. You don't need to rush into anything. Avoid the final sale mentality. This is a danger. This is an ultimatum. Don't fall for it. This is much too early. A good man will wait until you are comfortable with the arrangement.

# WRAP IT UP

He's in the bag. You're happily on your way home with that precious package in hand. Phew! Time for a cappuccino and a biscotti. Remember the biscotti? You bought them in the grocery store before you made your list. Indulge yourself and relax. Open the bags as you savor your coffee and congratulate yourself for a shopping spree well done. So far, so good. You can try him on a little later. You'll have plenty of time to see if he enhances your wardrobe.

The store usually gives you a reasonable amount of time to decide on your purchase. Within that period of time, you can return the item for a full cash refund. Cash refunds or full and immediate credits to your account are the best. Merchandise credits keep you shopping in the same place. You don't want that. There may be other intriguing stores that you have yet to explore. Make sure you can get a full refund.

Your full cash refund is a no loss agreement. You have not invested a great deal of time with him yet. You are dating and you are monogamous. You haven't bought the rings and set the forever after date. You didn't introduce him to your family. You are spending more time getting to know each other. There is no commitment and no decision on whether you will continue to see each other. So you are entitled to a full refund of your time and purchase. No signed agreement. No fees. No loss.

When you get your purchase home take it out of the bag, and try it on with your whole wardrobe again. Take your time. There's no rush. Sit with your cappuccino and biscotti. Take a breath. Get comfortable. Pull out the shoes you want to try, the dresses it may complement, and all of the items you thought would coordinate. Don't take off the tags. He isn't quite yours yet. You are still making a decision. Technically you're still shopping for a man.

Play with it for a while. See if you're happy with your new present. Try it on with as many clothes as you can. It may have more possibilities than you think. What about the brown suede jacket? Try it with the burgundy satin blouse. Does it go with boots as well as shoes? You're just frolicking. Try out the possibilities. Put your hair up. Do it casual and formal. See whether this really flatters you and puts you in your best light.

Dating is an exploration. Go out into the world. Meet people together. Go to different places and see how he responds to your environment, your favorite places and your friends. If you like to dance, get out there and go dancing together. If he likes sports, go to a game with him. Discover how you two get along in each other's world. This is what you do when you bring your purchase home. You try it on with all of the other outfits and accessories in your wardrobe. You can discover new things about each other and about yourself. That's part of the fun.

Still convinced this is a great deal? How do you know? Your friends like him well enough. He did fine at your bowling tournament. He was great at the ballet. He cheered your local team. He enjoys your home cooking as well as your favorite restaurant. You enjoy his friends well enough. You like going to flea markets looking for old tools. You are comfortable listening to his music. Sounds good so far.

By now, you've spent some quality time together and with your friends. You can see whether you both really get along, whether your conversations flow and whether you do enjoy each other's company. This still is not a final sale yet. But, you are getting close.

What's next? Take off the tags. Save them! Put them in your top drawer or your jewelry box. You still have time, but now you feel more confident about your purchase. The return policy gives you a decent amount of time to think about your purchase in a more relaxed setting. Don't rush or let yourself be rushed. This is an investment piece and it really is perfect and appropriate to take your time before the refund policy expires. Relax a bit. This has all been very exciting. Even though you were practical all the way, inside your heart was soaring with anticipation.

With all of this in mind, it's time to look at your shopping list again. Get into something cozy, pour yourself something soothing, and open that shopping list, the one with his name on it that you keep hidden away. You've been reviewing it all along, but now you have much more information. In the store, you examined every detail that you could. Now, it's in your hands. Look at all of the qualities you listed and see how he measures up. Be objective.

Follow the identical process you followed after your first few dates. Make check marks and notes next to all of the positive evidence. Check or star everything that is in line with your needs and desires. Bless those good points. You can have several checks and dates next to a quality that he continually displays. That's reliable confirmation of positive evidence of his good and desired qualities. This is why you made the purchase and brought him home.

Put question marks near the traits that are as yet unknown. You still have no evidence, but you'll be looking for it. The evidence hasn't shown up because circumstances have not presented themselves.

Put your X's and dates next to the qualities to track negative evidence. Cross out those areas where you can see a quality is missing. Give special thought to the areas where he receives demerits. Start to make more notes about these areas. If he did something significant that gives you negative evidence of a quality sorely missing, keep track. That's all you are doing and you need the intel. You need to pay attention to negative evidence, too. That's why you're shopping. Don't forget the Bonus Points. You want to know everything you can to make the best choices for your life and love.

Negative Evidence is not Negative Behavior. This is your life. There are no excuses for any type of negative, erratic or cruel behavior. There are no excuses for betrayal or dishonesty. This is your shopping list. The store doesn't have any excuse for not carrying the merchandise. This man doesn't have any excuses for bad or undesirable behavior. It's either on the list, missing or at fault.

So simple! That's why you are shopping. You have the power of the list. There are no excuses. You can forgive him for something minor, but don't overlook what he did. If you overlook it or minimize it, you're making an excuse for his behavior. There are no excuses for any type of behavior. When a person acts inappropriately, that is who they are. It can be a minor infraction due to stress. It can be a hidden pattern that will increase with time. There are traits and situations that are forgivable. There are traits and actions that are unforgiveable. That's all up to you. It can also mean that he has serious, destructive flaws. If you are complaining about things he does and says, that's a warning. Negative evidence shows you what's missing and what is wrong for you. Be clear what it is that you forgive. You can forgive anything that you want. It goes on the list all the same. Negative evidence must be included or you won't really know whether your list is working and you got what you need and want.

---

*Spend less time in the complaints department and more time at returns. If you're dating someone you complain about, just return him.*

Keeping track of positive evidence on your *Shopping For A Man* list is just as important. Give the guy full credit. If he is generous, kind, and honorable, give him check marks. If he goes beyond what you are used to or shows you more, put some stars on that list. We love Bonus Points. While most women tend to ignore, dismiss or prematurely forgive negative evidence, some women discount positive evidence. Don't discount or miss any of the extra wonderful things he does. Pay attention and acknowledge how he treats others and does extra special things for you. Always say thank you and acknowledge the blessings and gifts you receive from a great guy.

From now, until the refund period is over, refer to your shopping list as often as possible. Don't be obsessive.

Enjoy your time with him. This extension period can last anywhere from several weeks to many months. The refund policy is the time you need to make an accurate assessment of whether the fit, style and comfort work for you, complement you and enhance your life. Take all of the time that you need to make an insightful, clear assessment of your purchase. This is a relationship, but it's also a major purchase and investment. Right now, you are considering whether this relationship is what you want and if this man is going to enhance and complement your life.

There is still no lifetime commitment yet. Don't think there is and don't assume you know where this is going. Relax and enjoy. When you have a commitment, you have an emotional mortgage. It's like buying a house. You have agreements. You have responsibilities. Right now, you're a pre-approved shopper. You can really kick those tires and look under the hood, but you did not purchase the car. You are looking at the house, thinking that may be a great place to live and an excellent investment. This is the time to call in the qualified inspector (that's you) and check for termites, water damage, foundation problems and plumbing leaks. You are not ready to place a down payment and look for financing.

You and he are the only ones who can decide how much time is extended for a return of your merchandise. This is a joint venture. You are both exploring the possibilities and potential of having a long-term, monogamous, committed relationship. You're still not there. You know that he is going to be assessing the quality of his purchase, while you are assessing the quality of yours.

There is no set guideline for the time/satisfaction ratio. You have full power here. This extended period can be from four to six weeks all the way to six or more months. My suggestion for the time/satisfaction period is three months followed by a detailed review. What's your comfort zone? Are you impatient? Do you have to know right away? Are you willing to gracefully explore the view? Relax and enjoy this time together. See what develops and how it works. If you could go into the showroom, bring home a new car, try it out for a few months and then decide if you wanted to keep it, you'd have a great time. You'd take a few long trips. You'd really cruise. That's what you're doing right now.

A lot of this checking is fun. Play. Talk. Enjoy. Share. No commitment yet. Don't put any more money into this deal until all of the papers are signed. You haven't made your final commitment to this purchase. This is just a very long test drive.

You know you're fantasizing about happily-ever-after. Just don't believe it. You may imagine how your children will look, or what your wedding is going to be like, but it's just a dream right now. It may be a beautiful dream, but it has no solid foundation. Remember, you are still checking it out. Thank goodness you still have your shopping list, the tags and the receipt.

Sometimes women think that once they bring him home, that's it. It's a done deal. NO! You can take him back. You don't have to keep him if he doesn't fit in with your lifestyle. Enjoy this purchase. It's still refundable. At this stage you do not go into business together. Do not buy a house, car, horse or pet together. Ponder the possibilities. Just don't fool yourself into thinking you have to keep him, now that you brought him home. That's a myth. As long as you haven't been fooled into a final sale, you can always take him back.

---

*If it's not working,*
*just take him back for a refund.*

# REFUNDS AND RETURNS

What if he decides that this relationship is not working? He tells you that it's over. Guess what? It's over. Don't try to convince him that you are a great deal. He doesn't get it. It's a waste of time. Don't ask him why. Who cares? He has his value judgments. He has his own issues, standards and motives. He's exploring his ideas of a relationship, just as you are discovering yours. How great is this? He'll return himself. You don't even have to go back to the store. And there's still time for more shopping.

He may be tweed and you may be silk. What difference does it make if he decides that this doesn't work for him? You are not at fault. You're fabulous just as you are. There is nothing you can do or should do to alter yourself to fit his needs. Why would you want to do that? To please him? He isn't pleased enough right now, and no amount of changing will do that.

You are shopping. You are still shopping for a man. You do not have a full commitment to buy anything, because the time has not expired on your exchange agreement. You still have the tags and the receipt. He knows what he wants. It isn't you. Don't be upset. Do you really want a man that doesn't fully appreciate you? Who cares if he looks great? Do you really want a sweater that itches like crazy? Answer, NO!

He doesn't think you fit. Wonderful. He's not your man. It's so simple and easy. You had a great time shopping. You tried this one out and he wasn't it. Thank him. Let him go. He has saved you an amazing amount of time and work. He's even returning himself to the "Great Galactic Shopping Mall Of Love." Perfect. Now you have an even better shopping list.

It's your turn, or rather your return. He looked so cute in the store. Now, you're not so sure. The sweater bunches when you sit down. It falls into these rolls around your waist and you look ten pounds heavier. You tried it on with jeans. You tried it on with a cute leather skirt. It is just not working. Send it back. Take it right to the refund desk and get your money back now.

The comments that he made a few weeks ago were cute and witty. With time they are becoming biting and sarcastic. The conversations that were so intellectually stimulating initially are really just quotes from other people. He doesn't think for himself at all. You want to go out and have some fun.

You're getting to know him better. He's not what you expected. These may seem like minor infractions. Until you feel what's under them. Those biting and sarcastic comments about you are hurtful. You may not be overly sensitive. He may be doing it intentionally. He doesn't seem to care. He delights in it. Watch out. He is cruel. The more he gets to know you, the crueler he will get. Maybe he just does not have the same interests. There's nothing really wrong or annoying. He's just not fun or exciting for you. You're seeing more and realizing there are things you need that he doesn't provide and things he does that just don't sit well with you.

Looking at your shopping list will set things very clear in your mind. He may be too possessive. He may be too jealous. He may be detached. He may have interests that don't interest you at all. The important thing is what you want, not what he is. Pay attention. He is showing you who he is and how he enjoys his life. If it doesn't work for you, there's nothing else you need to do. The returns desk is on the third floor, second aisle to your right. Pack up that bundle and take the escalator. Take it back. They'll credit your refund right to your card.

***Your shoes need to complement your outfit.***
***Your man needs to complement your life.***

Your shopping list makes you a power shopper, if you pay attention to your list. One benefit to your shopping list is that you can see if you repeatedly choose the same type of man with bad results. When you're face to face with your man and your list, you can really clarify your mistakes. You can see whether he fulfills the qualities of the list or not. You can go right over everything and see whether you are paying attention or making excuses for his behavior. All of the qualities, all of the evidence is on the *Shopping For A Man* list right in front of you. How many times do you have to buy that brand of jeans that creep up the crotch to know they do not fit? They don't fit. They don't flatter. Buy another brand.

When your illusions are sitting on the couch with you, you have a greater chance of waking up. You can see what attracted you and where you went wrong. It's not his fault. You picked him. Maybe you keep looking for that dashing man. He looks so hot and everyone notices him. Then, you find out that he wants to be noticed, but he doesn't pay attention to you. Check your list for that. You may want to rethink that attribute.

If you keep choosing men who don't want to make a commitment, check your list. Did you really make notes on what he said and how he acted? Were you truthful with yourself? Did you write down that you want a man who will make a commitment to you? Is this really on your list and are you paying attention? Your list will tell you. Maybe you omitted something very important. This is great. What if you completely forgot an attribute that is really important? How can you check it or find evidence if you completely omitted it? Add it to your list right now. Maybe you're noticing you have things on your list that don't really matter to you. I'm not saying you should loosen up. I'm mentioning qualities that just don't matter to you. Just like when I added two qualities on my list that would please my mom. They didn't matter to me. Now is the time to reconsider them.

Sometimes things sneak up on you. Certain attributes may be so subtle that you didn't notice them. You thought you needed someone who paid a lot of attention to you, but this man is obsessive. You have no room to breathe. Great. Now you know more of what you want. Add a detail to your list. Upgrade it. That way you become more moderately attentive. Then, when you're looking for actions that show positive evidence, you can note the difference between the two. Maybe he was dishonest. You didn't see it right away because he avoided those issues. He was honest with you, but you found out later that he wasn't so ethical with your friends. He did something very minor, but a friend mentioned it to you. Maybe you need to know there is a difference between bragging and lying. You now have the clues. Put this detail on your list. This may be enough to get a refund. It may be something that you are going to watch. Now you're updating your list.

Look at all of the flashing lights. Listen to those warning bells. You can upgrade your ideas and your satisfaction levels by paying attention. When you see something that doesn't work for you, add a new attribute to your list. Make a note of what attribute you don't want and then write it in the positive. Make a note that you don't want someone who complains a lot. Write the positive. You want a man who is upbeat and confident. Sometimes you can add something that you don't want. Sometimes you add a new quality that you hadn't thought was important, but now is. If you haven't asked for a refund yet, but noticed something missing, you can see if he has positive evidence of that quality. If not, you can go shopping and get it.

If you're not getting what you want, this list will show you where you go wrong. Isn't that great? You have a shopping consultant at your command. Just read the traits and see what you tend to overlook. It is in big bold letters. You wrote it. You may have everything on your list to shop for the perfect man, but continually overlook the very obvious facts. Maybe you omitted several very important qualities. When you are smiling deeply into the eyes of a missing clue, you have a better chance of seeing it.

*"Take it from a guy: If you're in love with somebody, you will swim the stream, you will climb the mountain, you will slay the dragon. You're going to get to her somehow, some way."*
*Phil McGraw*

# IT'S A DEAL!
# OR IS IT AN ORDEAL?

You decided. You both decided. Congratulations to you. It's a deal. This is the point of no return. The time periods for any refunds expired and you are deep into a marvelous relationship. What a gift.

You found the man of your dreams. He is nearly everything you looked for and has extra bonuses as well. Congratulations.

The clearest guideline for a true deal is a total agreement for commitment. It's important to have specific guidelines for a deal. When you purchase a car, once the papers are signed it is yours. There are no refunds. You have a commitment to care for the car, get the insurance, fill it with gas, pay attention to all auto maintenance and obey all the road safety rules when you drive.

Be clear on the standards of a deal. Just like that dress you bought, a deal is a permanent purchase. You have no intention of an exchange. You threw away the receipt. The tags are long gone. You do not plan to take it back to the store eight months later because it just didn't work out. A deal is a final agreement. He has no intention of leaving for greener horizons. You have no intention of trying it a little longer to see if it works. It is a done deal. Case closed. The end.

A deal is total commitment and responsibility. If you don't have a total commitment and responsibility, you are still in possible refund land or you decided you don't really care. This isn't a judgment about you, but you have to know when a deal is a deal. A deal is not an assumption. This is not potential. This is not a "we'll see." This is a full and total commitment, the way you want it. This means he says he loves you, he makes a commitment to you, you say yes, and the date and agreement is set. This is an explicit and decisive deal. You have evidence. You have formed a mutually exclusive relationship that leads to a full commitment. This is a definite deal. This is a total commitment, commitment, commitment. Congratulations.

---

*You know you got a deal*
*when your guy is better than you asked for.*

*You know it's an ordeal*
*when you're still struggling to find joy together.*

# WHAT IS AN ORDEAL?

What's an ordeal? An ordeal is not having a real deal. An ordeal is extending the time with the illusion of a deal, but not the agreement. An understanding about your love together is not a deal. An intuition that this one may lead to a committed relationship is not a deal. A conversation that one day you will get married is not a deal. A pledge to love you forever is not a deal. All of this is an ordeal, if you want a long-term, committed, monogamous relationship.

A decision to live together is not a deal. Maybe it's a lease. And if that is what works for you, then it's perfect. You have to know what works for you and what you both really want. You are still in the exchange period. You decided to live together. Now you are. To be gracious, you can call this deal pending or a lease with an option to buy. Great. This is an interim formal agreement. That means you are as close to a deal as you can get, but the deal is not finalized. The negotiations are not firm. The details are still in flux. You still have the receipt. The back door may be closed, but it isn't locked. There is no firm commitment to culminate this arrangement. Unless you personally decide you will never marry because of your own philosophy about the institution of marriage itself, this is not a deal.

If you are really sure that you never want to marry because of your personal philosophy on the subject, fine. You still have to formalize the transaction. A different kind of commitment is needed. It may not be the paper of matrimony, but you still want something concrete. It's important to know whether you are really together or in a very long and extended refund agreement. You need to know and create what constitutes a deal, if it's not marriage.

---

"Unless a commitment is made, there are only promises and hopes; but no plans."
Peter F. Drucker

You may be monogamous. You may be in a relationship where both of you decided to see each other exclusively. That does not make it a deal. There are many facets to the dating dance. As your love and relationship grows, the feelings and commitment mirrors that development. To have a deal, you must have a specific commitment. You need a 'by when.' "You love me, you want us to live together, and eventually get married. By when? When will this transpire?" When you have the answer, you have the deal. All sales are final after the return date.

Don't worry if you realize that you really don't have a deal yet. You can be in test drive mode for as long as you like. You are breaking up more illusions about commitment. This can take getting used to. Most people think that saying 'I love you' means commitment. It doesn't. It means that he loves you. That's lovely and wonderful, but it's not a deal and it's not a commitment. He and you have to agree about your being in a long-term, permanent relationship. When you are clear about the real implications of a bonded, monogamous relationship, you know when you have one. Your shopping list shows you what you want. The gleaming gold on your ring finger shows you that you got it.

You don't have to do anything about this, either. You don't have to worry that it hasn't happened. You can be patient and continue to explore this romance. You can enjoy the special relationship and see what develops. Give yourself permission to celebrate the coming together of two people. No pressure here and make sure you don't put that pressure on yourself or on him. This is about what you want to create and how you want to live, not whether you closed the deal.

You may not know if you even want to finalize that purchase, so don't push yourself into it if you have some doubts. There are many aspects to consider when you make a solid commitment. If you need more time, take it. It doesn't matter what people think. Relax. Bask in his company and when you are ready, you will be very clear if it's a deal or not.

Some deals take longer than others. You have your time frame and he has his. Who knows which of you will be ready first? If you have already discussed your need and intention for a permanent relationship, then he knows what you want. To get this far, he has specifically told you that he wants the same bond. Right now, you haven't agreed that the bond will be between the two of you.

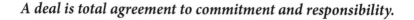

*A deal is total agreement to commitment and responsibility.*

Just breathe and look within yourself. It's not about how fast you close the deal. It's whether this is the guy you want, that he has the qualities that light you up and the two of you can really see your relationship in the long term. If you don't really see this as a long-term commitment and journey together, you can choose to continue as is, as long as you really know that this is not a deal. Don't keep on sliding forward, but make that choice. If you don't want something formal and real, then be very clear you made that choice. It's not a deal. It's a decision. If you do want a deal, if you do want a long-term, committed, monogamous relationship with this man, if you are really ready for the commitment, the marriage, etc. Then see if this is the guy.  Go to your list and make sure you are clear that this is what you want and that you are ready for that deal. Then, you better make sure that he is ready, too. When everything gets to yes, that is a deal. When the formal commitment is in place, clearly agreed upon by both of you, this is a deal! Fabulous!

# RECOGNIZE THE FOUR PRIMARY STALL TACTICS

Sometimes, you really don't know that the dating and relationship are stalled. It's going along, but not going forward. Not going anywhere. That was happening to a good friend of ours. She was dating a guy for a while. Seemed fine, but when she kept on talking about commitment and marriage, somehow the conversation was too vague. We'd talked about this many times, and she wanted a man's opinion, not mine. So she had a conversation with my husband, Peter. The three of us sat together and Peter listened to her whole story. Then he smiled and said something that shocked her.

*"When a guy wants a beer, he gets a beer.
Guys know how to go after what they want.
For a man, dating is that simple."*
Peter Bried

The different changes on her face were adorable. Surprise, confusion, shock and then laughter.

She nodded. "It's not going to happen is it?" Peter shook his head and said, "No." She knew the relationship was going nowhere and actually, she took it really well. "When a guy wants a beer, he gets a beer," was her rallying cry to all her single women who would ask if she thought their relationships were going anywhere.

Just in case you don't have the deal yet, it's best to know why. Stall Tactics are primary indicators that no deal is in place yet. It may even indicate that there is not going to be a deal. Stalling means different things. You have to determine what it means and if there is an appropriate action to take. It could be that you are stalling or that he is stalling. What's going on?

### THE CLASSIC STALL
You hit a definite plateau. Everything seems to be at a standstill. The next move for you is a serious commitment and a decision to be together. You know this is not just dating to you. You are in the stages of falling deeply in love. If he isn't going to proclaim something, you need to know. You want to know if this is the relationship to stand the test of time. There is no forward motion. Any conversations about a bonded relationship seem to circle around like buzzards without their prey. There's no conclusion. There is no 'yes' or 'no'. You have fun, enjoy each other's company and feel comfortable with each other. Is this going anywhere?

In the classic stall there are signs of great possibility, but no clear affirmation. You don't want to float around in this romance if there is no permanent outcome. You know what you want. You want the whole package. You don't want to buy half a pair of gloves. You don't want one shoe. You want it all.

Whether the actual conversation that confronts this dilemma has transpired or not, those deep stirrings and doubts are churning the waters. Maybe you feel those doubts and then let them subside when you are together. Maybe you think about it all of the time. Whatever the process, you recognize there is a next step. You just don't know if you will take that next step together. You don't know if he is really ready, willing and able to say 'yes' to the deal.

Now, if it's you who is stalling and not him, then go back to your list. Are you unsure? Are you afraid? Where are your doubts and fears? Are you unsure of him and your love? Are you unsure of yourself and maybe your own level of a total commitment to another person?

I know you dream about putting that shopping list away. Then you won't have to wonder if it's a deal. Oh, no. Not yet. Remember, you can have it all! You know what it is you want and you are in the last stages of getting it. You're getting itchy to throw away the receipts and really play big. That's great. Check your shopping list and examine the evidence. See it clearly and make a choice, deal or no deal.

## THE WORST CASE STALL

He never really wanted a commitment. He lied. He didn't realize that he had unresolved issues. He was in this relationship because you were great and treated him well. He was comfortable and, unless you force the issue, what you have now is what you get.

This is the worst case stall. He isn't a deal and was never ever going to be one. It doesn't matter about his potential. Who cares if he's a good catch? He's uncatchable. When you discover this, you may be angry, hurt or confused. Don't delve into why he didn't want you. He may not want anyone for very long. He may be a Power Shopper. You're getting amazing results. Even if this particular transaction was not exactly what you wanted, at least you know it. You know that he doesn't have certain qualifications. Now you know what those qualifications are, and you know how to get them. What do you do? You go shopping!

Look at your list again and again. What did you check off that was a mistake? Did you give him the benefit of the doubt just because he was so cute? Here's one of my favorite statements.

### *There is no benefit to the doubt.*

I received that spiritual guidance in a meditation a long time ago. I love it. The benefit of the doubt means you forget about your doubts about a situation and give the other person the benefit. The benefit is that you ignore your doubts, do not act on them and just wait. The only person you doubted was yourself. Not a good move. He has to prove that he's worthy. What did you selectively ignore because you wanted someone around? What did you omit? What did you overlook about him? Being desperate leads you into stupidity. If you saw some fatal flaws that you discretely decided to ignore, you are cheating yourself. You are shopping for a man. Be a Power Shopper.

Did you have real evidence of the qualities you said were there? Evidence is a clear and specific example. Review the qualities you said that he had and decide if your assessment was accurate. This is a great time to beef up your shopping skills. You can see how well you've done so far and what else you found out about yourself. Now you can see the difference between false advertising and accurate descriptions. Now you can increase your shopping skills and be even more fastidious about the evidence of qualities, compatibility and your own needs.

There are more reasons for stalling than blatant dishonesty. The worst case stall is not just on him. You may be the one who is stalling. You may not be quite ready. You can almost imagine life together as a unit, but not quite. You may need more time. Check this and see. It's not just cold feet. The worst case stall reveals you really don't want this. It reveals whether you've been fooling yourself or him. Please take a close look.

A lot of people look for bells, whistles and marching bands to make a decision. They may come or they may not. They may be there and they may pass. The dramatic ecstasy of a relationship gives way to a richer field of love. Lust is great, but every man's little lust meter goes up and down. Love encompasses more than passion and joy. When love is full in a relationship you live within it, it doesn't only reside within you.

If you're still unsure after all of this shopping and examining, it may be time for a solid conversation. If you both want a committed relationship, it's time to talk. This is not a philosophical conversation about the benefits of marriage in the great social structure of the world. This is a conversation about the two of you. What is there? Why are you hesitating? Is there something either of you feel is missing? Are you both frightened? Do you have unresolved issues about family, career, religion, dreams, children and life?

Issues must be sorted out. Even though it may mean a parting of the ways, it could just as easily mean a coming together. You may be looking at that chocolate brown suit, just wishing it had sterling silver buttons and a little more topstitching. Then, you think, it would be perfect. You'd buy it in a snap. Would you? Or would you find that the topstitching was really in the wrong shade of brown and the sterling buttons were bigger than you imagined? No one is going to be everything to you or for you. Be realistic in what will add to your happiness.

A relationship isn't going to make you happy. You share happiness in your relationship. Marriages and committed relationships are dedicated to resolving the issues that come up. Life throws more issues at you, even when you think you have handled the very last one. Maybe you don't really need those silver buttons. Why not try adding a large vintage sterling brooch to the lapel? You may have more versatility with your outfit and your relationship if you know that you can always add new things to it.

## THE FEAR STALL

Stalling out of fear is confusing. In the fear stall, you don't know why you're not ready. He pulls back in every conversation about commitment. You end up avoiding the issue as much as you can. But there it is, making faces at you in the background. It reminds you it's there, and you can't stand to look at it again. This is fear. This is different than recognizing negative evidence and realizing you cannot make a commitment. You are stalling because of fear. Ask yourself, "What you are afraid to see?" If it isn't you, ask him the same question. If you can't talk about this, you may have trouble making bigger decisions in the future.

It's like a sumptuous chocolate cake. You know you want it. You're salivating at the smooth deep color, the moist rich texture. There are shaved chocolate curls on the top and special icing. You know it's filled with fresh sliced raspberries that will be tart and sweet when you take your first bite. It's in the baker's glass case and you know he's one of the best bakers in town. What's holding you back?

All of your conversations about cake are holding you back. It's too rich. Think of how fattening it must be. It has so much sugar and the media has warned everyone one that sugar could be bad for you. Then your mind accelerates. Everywhere you look, you see five hundred pound women, walking the streets with tears in their eyes, and slices of this chocolate cake in their hands. You see little starving children all over the world praying for a slice of that good chocolate cake. You hear your mother warning you about chocolate cake. Your friends remind you about the times they went through chocolate cake withdrawal. You see your tombstone. It says, "If only she hadn't eaten that chocolate cake."

This is fear. You are in the fear stall. Your mind is providing you with every possible exaggerated reason for not having what you really want. You really want the cake! Calm down. None of these fears are rational. There is no basis for any of these thoughts. So what if your last relationship didn't work out? So what if your ten-year marriage failed? So what if your friends are jealous? The past is the past. Your fears are there to let you know what is standing in your way. Most fears are unfounded and irrational.

What is a real fear? You're at your front door. It's a screen door and it's open. Crap! There's a ferocious lion on the other side of the door. He's looking at you and growling. All you have in your hand is a fly swatter. The lion is ready to pounce. That's a very real fear. Everything else is dread and worry.

You don't have to repeat the past. You have your list, and you're checking it more than twice. You want this one. You want to throw away the tags and receipts, put on the dress and go dancing. Your fears about what life could hold, based on what you've already gone through, are holding you back. They're just fears. None of them are real. So what if you have fears that aren't real? So, what if you just eat the cake? You will have the most delicious cake ever imagined. Woman, eat the cake!

## THE GENERIC STALL

You both talked about commitment. You agree it's the right thing to do. No one will make a move in that direction. You have doubts.

He has doubts. It's time to up the ante. No one has actually said they want to end the relationship, but it has most definitely stalled. You wait and wait, hoping for a shift. It isn't there yet. Time to get into gear. You are really stalled.

This is a generic stall. You are stalled with doubts. It's nothing overwhelming and nothing insurmountable. You have some doubts. He has some doubts. These doubts are not significant enough for a refund.

Set your own time deadline. Decide that you have one month, two months, no more than three months to decide, "Is this a go or a no?" Don't bother to reflect on the reasons for a stall. Sometimes cars just do that. There may not be anything wrong. You could've hit the gas by accident. It could be too hot. It doesn't matter. Shift that car and move it.

You may want to tell him that you both have one month to decide where this relationship will take you. This is a personal deadline. No sense in sitting around for five more months in the same outfit waiting for a party that may never come. You may never get an invitation. It may sound like an ultimatum. That's nice. A deadline is the span of time you have to decide. There is a deadline on returns. There is a deadline on filing taxes. There is a deadline to waiting for this relationship to move forward.

If he gets crazy, you know his answer. If he makes a scene, says you're pressuring him and gets angry, he already said, "no." If he asks to think about it, then let him. He still could say, "no," but you gave him a certain amount of time to think. He may very well say, "yes." If the deadline comes up and he says, "yes," and you freak, guess what. You can say, "no," too.

The point is you have to know if you really bought the merchandise. You want to know if this is a deal or not. You may come to realize that you don't want a committed relationship. You just don't want to buy anything. You want a rental. You want a long-term lease. You may even want a lease with an extended option to buy. Good. Amend your list. Now you know what you want and you can shop for that.

Decide what's important for you. You are the shopper. If you don't want to buy it, smile at the clerk and say, "Just browsing." If you really want to buy something, go for it. If he is there and willing, pull out the cash and lay your money on the table. If he's not willing or able, put away your wallet, close your purse and go to another store. There's probably a wonderful man in the jewelry section, looking at the wedding rings, hoping and wondering if 'she' will ever come along.

# IT REALLY IS A DEAL!

Congratulations. You decided to go the distance. You have a fully, agreed upon commitment that you both know is right. You have a solid, loving relationship that speaks to your hearts, addresses your style and celebrates your love and life together. Yes! Congratulations! You have a deal!

It's time to complete the transaction. That's your choice. What does complete mean to you? Is complete the white gown and the wedding cake? Is complete a home and bedroom furniture? Is complete a ring and a gathering of friends? To have the deal, you have to agree to the terms and formalize that agreement. You've been shopping for a man, and so you must have thought about this, discussed it and agreed. You know what a deal is and what it means to you. Be honest. There's a lot of room for personal evaluation in this final stage. Be very clear what a sale means to you and to him.

### NOW IT'S DETAIL TIME.

What does a full time, bonded, committed, monogamous, forever-after relationship look like to you? What does it look like to him? I feel very romantic about this. You are creating a loving future together.

How do you complete the transaction in this amazing, "Great Galactic Shopping Mall Of Love"? You examine your deeper needs and dreams and share them with him. Ask him what he wants. You both discussed it earlier, now you are making it real. Be clear. You create your future in this conversation. Speak what you want. Listen to what he feels. Make sure that everything about the purchase is out in the open. Once you know and understand the details and you know what the transaction really is and you and he agree, you finally negotiated the deal. Next, you need a symbol of that deal and commitment.

"A ring means a commitment.
But more than that, it means that you've talked
about your shared future and have
decided together on a shared vision of it."
Patti Stanger

You have a ring or a gorgeous token of the bond. This is a bonus for shopping, too. There is a reason why engagement rings are gold or platinum with diamonds or sapphires, emeralds or rubies. Gold and platinum never break down. They don't deteriorate. They last and shine forever and they hold their value and often increase in value over time. Precious gems like diamonds and sapphires are the most precious gemstones in the world. They last forever. They have a hard crystalline structure that lasts millions of years. They hold their value and show true worth and appreciation. This ring and gemstone show the promise of the deal. This engagement ring finalizes the commitment to a future. The wedding rings of gold or platinum will come and they are the final bond. They are the ultimate symbol of that agreement. I say get jewelry. Jewelry is something you will wear and cherish and it is a great symbol of endless love and commitment.

All you need now is the date. When is this purchase finalized? You decide. Will it be next week? Are you going to Las Vegas to be married by an Elvis impersonator? Are you going to have a formal, white dress, classic wedding? Are you making plans to marry in a year or so in a full huge ceremony? Are you going to be handfasted in an ancient Celtic ceremony? Did you decide to dispense with convention and live together forever? When is all of this taking place? You need a specific date.

After this, if life gives you her blessings and everyone is clear, your deal is complete. You decide whether engagement, wedding or living together is the final deal.

Once you finalized the deal, get out that bottle of champagne. Lift your crystal glasses high and toast yourselves. You are A

Shopping Queen. You successfully completed shopping for a man.

Congratulations. You are a *Shopping For A Man* success. You receive the golden crown award for supreme shopping skills. Walk down that rich red carpet. Raise your sceptre high in the air. Wave to the admiring crowds. Hear the cheers and applause. You graduated *Shopping For A Man* with the highest honors. You finalized the deal. Plan the party, invite your friends, and give that great guy a big kiss! I wish you many blessings of love, harmony, partnership, fulfillment and years of joy together.

***And, drop me a line. Send me an email.***
***I want to congratulate you!***

## YOUR HAPPILY EVER AFTER DEAL TO HAVE AND TO HOLD

Ding. Ding. Ding. The bells are ringing. The champagne is flowing. The confetti and rose petals are cascading around you. This is it! You did it. You have your Happily Ever After Deal, to Have and To Hold. And congratulations to that fabulous man you discovered. You became a consummate consumer. You shopped for a man and you succeeded.

Now you are ready to have a great life together.
How did you achieve such brilliant success?

### You honored yourself and you honored your guy.
Remember what I said in the Introduction? You honored yourself and you honored your guy. You didn't tell the guy you're dating about your shopping list and this book. Honor is key to a true loving, long lasting relationship. If there's no honor then there's nothing to build upon. Without honor for yourself and each other, then love is weak. When honor is reciprocal in your relationship you can build a fabulous life together. This is about you. This was the first thing you did to achieve success in *Shopping For A Man*.

### You broke apart *The Six Illusions of Commerce.*

That means that you shattered your feelings and beliefs of scarcity.
You let go of the illusions that you have to settle to have a man and
a relationship, that you're not good enough or that men have all the
power in the dating game. You are not settling for faulty goods and
damaged materials. Yes! A life partner is not a discounted, fire sale
item. He's the "go to" classic in your wardrobe. He is the foundation
of the best style you can imagine.

### You Cleaned *The Closets.*

You no longer have those worn out and obsolete ideas from your
past. You no longer live your life from hand-me-down criteria of
romance and love. You succeeded in TOSS. HOLD. KEEP. And you
eliminated the scuffed shoes, the ripped blouses and the really bad
ideas you had about men and relationships.

Now, you have a closet that is wide open and clean. You have
a closet where everything is known and accessible. You know what
you have and you've taken full responsibility for who you are and
how you create a relationship. Walking into a clean, well-ordered
closet is like heaven. And you have the heavenly man to prove it.

### You made your *Shopping For A Man List.*

This is huge. Your *Shopping for a Man* list is a critical component
of getting what you want, what you need and what will really work
for you. It's also a revelation in who you are. The list is a process of
self-discovery. You acknowledged and clarified your personal taste.
In shopping for a man, you did discover what you need and also
what you thought you needed, but actually didn't need at all. Brava!
This list will continue to show you so much about yourself and your
man.

And, if you want to know, I still have my list. Yes! I still have the *Shopping For A Man* list that I created and filled out when I first met and later married my husband. Now, it's a sacred reminder of all the wonderful qualities he has and the truly great guy that he is every day of my life.

And every so often, I add notes and dates. I add new, wonderful qualities I didn't notice before and I do this just to remind myself how great he is. And how great a shopper I am.

While you were shopping for a man you learned the vital skills of shopping and some pretty good ones you can use in general life.

### *You learned Browsing and Scanning mode.*
You learned how to just peruse the scene and see, without needing to make a commitment until much later. You learned all of the clues and became a smart shopper. You saw the Nine Signs of Fabulous and Flawed. You went through the racks and looked for positive and negative evidence. You looked for and discovered the bad signs, demerits and the bonus points.

### *Then, to reward your success, it was off the rack and into your hands.*

And Shopping Queen that you have become, you read the labels. Now you know you do fit well together. You know he is a quality guy. You checked the label for Care Instructions to make sure he can care for you and you can care for him. Relationships are mutual and in this loving union care and attention is vital for a lasting relationship that goes beyond the fads and endures a lifetime.

### *Next, it was into the Dressing Room.*
That was the final test of your newly developed *Shopping For A Man* skills. You noticed and followed each detail of a great fit, true colors and personal style. You didn't quit. You didn't settle for a cheap knock-off of a guy, a poser, an imposter of a man who isn't in it for the long term. You went for the real deal.

### *You did it!*
You are a success and you have the great guy and the relationship to prove it. You finalized the deal.

# Congratulations!
# YOU ARE A SHOPPING QUEEN!

Now you have a great man who is available only to you! He is a real man who loves you madly, who wants this relationship with you and only you. He appreciates you and all of your qualities. He knows how lucky he is to be sharing his life with you and he is happy to let you know how much he cares. He supports you in your life and your dreams. He honors you, listens to you and he is honest.

Your *Shopping For A Man* is complete. And that's what you want. Relax and share your love and life with this really fabulous man. Listen to him and share with him. Create a wonderful love and life together. Share your lives in love, support, joy, honor and dedication with each other.

Appreciate and acknowledge every moment of your love together. I have a very special secret to share with you. It's something I do every day. I always say, "I love you" and mean it. The first words I say to my husband in the morning are, "I love you." The very last words I say to my husband at night are, "I love you." That's the way we start and end every day. We don't take our love for granted and we don't overlook the blessings and the magic. I wish you the same.

*"It's all about love. We're either in love, dreaming about love, recovering from it, wishing for it or reflecting on it."*
*Michael Buble*

*One last thing ...*

*If you want love, you should have the best love -
conscious, strong, supportive and delightful love.*

*Have an empowered conversation about being a
woman and what is truly possible in the world.*

*You want friends and loved ones to be happy,
loved and fulfilled in all areas of their lives.*

*If you enjoyed this book and it shifted your thinking
or inspired you or simply made you laugh,
share the love and give a copy to a friend.*

*We need more love in the world.*

# ABOUT THE AUTHOR

L UMARI is a gifted internationally acclaimed intuitive life coach, psychic consultant, wisdom teacher, vibrational healer, visionary energy master and bestselling author who has shown thousands of people how to celebrate their soul purpose, follow their highest destiny, fulfill their dreams and Live Inspired.

With clients all over the world, she is passionate about providing guidance and sharing wisdom that creates transformation, fulfillment and inspiration for positive personal, professional and planetary change.

Enjoying a successful career as a sculptor, Lumari integrated her creative gifts as an artist with her powerful intuitive gifts of vision, channeling and communication to relentlessly follow her vision. Because of her extraordinary intuitive gifts, vibration and wisdom, Lumari is joyful vortex of inspiration. She opens the doors to your inner being. Her world class coaching provides the clarity, guidance and healing you need to fulfill your soul expression, soar in spirit, access opportunities and manifest greater wealth and success. Her insight, vibration and vision help you be the joyful soul and spirit you know you are inside and guide you to courageous success.

Her books, meditations and spiritual training workshops bring joyful awakening, profound clarity, spiritual connection and healing. They reveal secret teachings to raise awareness and Divine connection.

Her podcast the "Cosmic Coffee Break" brings enlightening meditations, wisdom teachings and interviews to share the vibrations to uplift your life and our world.

To Live Inspired, contact Lumari at LUMARI.com

# Also by Bestselling Author LUMARI

Do you Love Meditations and
Wisdom Teachings?

Check out and Subscribe to my
Cosmic Coffee Break podcast

CosmicCoffeeBreak.com
on iTunes and more

For more books, meditations, products
and resources
visit LUMARI.com

# BOOKS FROM LUMARI

## SHOPPING FOR A MAN JOURNAL

This is the companion to Lumari's book, Shopping For A Man. Your journal is your journey to joy, fulfillment and shopping to help you find and date that great guy, that amazing man, The One.

## LIVING INSPIRED WITH LUMARI

In this book, Lumari breaks apart the myths that rob you of the true vibrations of living inspired. She reveals the ART of Living Inspired, so you can create your own illumination and positive purpose every moment.

## AKASHIC RECORDS

Learn about the Akashic Records and the Beings who hold the Wisdom of the Ages. Lumari is the first to interview and channel direct communication with the Akashic. Discover who the Akashic Records are, how their system of Universal wisdom really works and how to achieve a connection of your own.

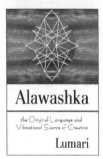

## ALAWASHKA

Discover the nature of Creation, the evolution of humanity and the power of Alawashka, the original language of Creation. Channeled by Lumari, the words, energies and wisdom in this book contain vibrations of universal transformation and can initiate your passage into higher consciousness, just by reading it.

# BOOKS FROM LUMARI

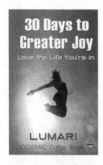

## 30 DAYS TO GREATER JOY

In this book, Lumari breaks apart the myths that rob you of the true vibrations of living inspired. She reveals the ART of Living Inspired, so you can create your own illumination and positive purpose every moment.
Paperback and audiobook.

## BREATHING MAGIC

Learn about the Beings who hold the Wisdom of the Ages. Lumari is the first to interview and channel direct communication with the Akashic. Discover who the Akashic Records are and how to achieve a connection of your own.
Paperback and audiobook.

Set the tone and energy for your shopping
and dating success.

Download your FREE
READY TO SHOP visualization

ShoppingForaMan.com

76403675R00148

Made in the USA
Columbia, SC
08 September 2017